CYCLING THE CAMINO DE SANTIAGO

CYCLING THE CAMINO DE SANTIAGO

THE WAY OF ST JAMES – CAMINO FRANCÉS

by Mike Wells

JUNIPER HOUSE, MURLEY MOSS,
OXENHOLME ROAD, KENDAL, CUMBRIA LA9 7RL
www.cicerone.co.uk

Printed in Czechia on responsibly sourced paper on behalf of Latitude Press Ltd
A catalogue record for this book is available from the British Library.
All photographs are by the author unless otherwise stated.

Route mapping by Lovell Johns www.lovelljohns.com
Contains OpenStreetMap.org data © OpenStreetMap
contributors, CC-BY-SA. NASA relief data courtesy of ESRI

Updates to this Guide

While every effort is made by our authors to ensure the accuracy of guide-books as they go to print, changes can occur during the lifetime of an edition. Any updates that we know of for this guide will be on the Cicerone website (www.cicerone.co.uk/969/updates), so please check before planning your trip. We also advise that you check information about such things as transport, accommodation and shops locally. Even rights of way can be altered over time.

The route maps in this guide are derived from publicly available data, databases and crowd-sourced data. As such they have not been through the detailed checking procedures that would generally be applied to a published map from an official mapping agency, although naturally we have reviewed them closely in the light of local knowledge as part of the preparation of this guide.

We are always grateful for information about any discrepancies between a guidebook and the facts on the ground, sent by email to updates@cicerone.co.uk or by post to Cicerone, Juniper House, Murley Moss, Oxenholme Road, Kendal, LA9 7RL.

Register your book: To sign up to receive free updates, special offers and GPX files where available, register your book at www.cicerone.co.uk.

Front cover: The Alto del Perdón, where 'the path of the wind crosses that of the stars' (Stage 3)

CONTENTS

Galicia

Santa María church in Viana (Stage 4)

Burgos has the greatest provision of dedicated cycle tracks of any Spanish city (Stage 7)

ROUTE SUMMARY TABLE

Stage	Start	Finish
1	St Jean-Pied-de-Port	Roncesvalles
2	Roncesvalles	Pamplona
3	Pamplona	Estella
4	Estella	Logroño
5	Logroño	Santo Domingo de la Calzada
6	Santo Domingo de la Calzada	Villafranca Montes de Oca
7	Villafranca Montes de Oca	Burgos
8	Burgos	Castrojeriz
9	Castrojeriz	Carrión de los Condes
10	Carrión de los Condes	Sahagún
11	Sahagún	León
12	León	Astorga
13	Astorga	Ponferrada
14	Ponferrada	O Cebreiro
15	O Cebreiro	Sarria
16	Sarria	Palas de Rei
17	Palas de Rei	Arzúa
18	Arzúa	Santiago de Compostela
Total	**St Jean-Pied-de-Port**	**Santiago de Compostela**

Camino route			Road route			Page
Distance (km)	Ascent (m)	Descent (m)	Distance (km)	Ascent (m)	Descent (m)	
28	1106	345	27.5	961	200	**50**
42.5	491	982	46.5	316	807	**58**
45	814	848	48.5	704	738	**69**
48.5	863	904	46	660	701	**81**
50	797	540	49.5	623	366	**93**
34	579	274	33.5	540	235	**105**
38.5	406	493	36	292	379	**113**
40	327	368	51.5	376	417	**123**
43.5	323	301	45	232	210	**132**
39	216	219	42	233	236	**141**
55	258	253	54.5	253	248	**148**
47.5	346	316	48	325	295	**160**
54	824	1150	54.5	801	1127	**172**
53	1046	285	54.5	988	227	**182**
38	611	1479	44.5	373	1241	**194**
47	943	827	47.5	914	798	**203**
28	431	595	29.5	460	624	**213**
38.5	739	869	39	566	696	**221**
770km	**11,120m**	**11,048m**	**798km**	**9617m**	**9545m**	

The kindly image of Santiago Peregrino over the Door of Pardon in Santiago cathedral (Stage 18)

INTRODUCTION

Navarrete in the Rioja wine region has 11 bodegas (wineries) (Stage 5)

When a ninth-century Galician shepherd found the long-buried body of the Apostle James in a remote corner of north-west Spain, he could not have envisaged that his discovery would lead to a huge pilgrimage with hundreds of thousands of people making their way every year across Europe to visit his find – or that this pilgrimage would witness not one but two periods of popularity, with 500 years between them. The first pilgrimage, which ran between the ninth and sixteenth centuries was a hard journey. Medieval *peregrinos* (pilgrims) would travel thousands of kilometres to Santiago with no maps or guides, in basic clothing, braving the weather,

dangerous animals, thieves and polluted drinking water to gain absolution from their sins by touching what believers claim to be the tomb of Santiago (St James), a disciple of Jesus Christ. When they reached Santiago, they had to turn around and retrace the hazardous journey. They could be away from home for up to a year, with no way of contacting family and friends. Significant numbers would never return home, some dying enroute and others settling down for a new life in northern Spain.

The journey is much easier for modern pilgrims. They can travel in weatherproof clothing on well-waymarked trails, drinking safely from countless drinking fountains that are tested frequently to guarantee water purity, with neither wolf, bear nor robber in sight. Every night they can stay in basic but comfortable *albergues* (pilgrim hostels) and consume good-value filling food and wine from pilgrim menus in a wide choice of restaurants. They can use mobile phones to call home every night and post online pictures of themselves on their journey. When they reach Santiago, they can fly home effortlessly in a few hours.

The degree of hardship may have changed, but the journey is still one of discovery, both of new places and of the inner self. The route followed may have altered slightly but it still has the same name, El Camino de Santiago (The Way of St James) or usually just 'The Camino'. Medieval

pilgrims either walked or travelled on horseback. Modern pilgrims still walk, but very few use a horse. Those that do ride nowadays favour a bicycle and take approximately two weeks to complete the journey across northern Spain from St Jean to Santiago and it is for these cycling pilgrims that this guide has been written.

There is more than one pilgrim route to Santiago, but the most popular in medieval times and again today is the Camino Francés, named for the large number of French pilgrims who followed this route. Pilgrims started at many points throughout France or further afield, using different routes that converged upon St Jean-Pied-de-Port at the foot of the lowest and easiest pass over the Pyrenees into Spain. Their approximately 800km route from St Jean to Santiago follows

Rich medieval pilgrims travelled on horseback, nowadays only a handful use animal power (Stage 5)

a generally east–west trajectory, south of and parallel with the Cantabrian mountains. Beyond the Pyrenees the trail undulates through Navarre then crosses the wine-producing region of Rioja. After steadily ascending then descending into Burgos, the route reaches and crosses the northern tip of the meseta, a vast area of rolling high-level chalk downland that occupies much of central Spain. After León, the forested Montes de León and fertile Bierzo basin are crossed before the rolling green hills and valleys of Galicia are reached. The Camino ends at the great religious city of Santiago de Compostela, where the tomb of St James housed inside an 11th-century cathedral is the ultimate destination of the pilgrimage.

The Camino is not just a two-week ride through northern Spain. About half of walking peregrinos make the pilgrimage for religious reasons. For them the journey can become a voyage of self-discovery with the opportunity to meet and talk to like-minded believers, visit and perhaps take communion in ancient churches and cathedrals, while having time to contemplate the spiritual side of their lives. Others, including many cyclists, make the journey for exercise and recreation. For them the challenge is to successfully cycle 800km including traverses of the Pyrenees and the Montes de León. Yet more are attracted by the cultural side of the Camino, seeking to visit stunning cathedrals, historic abbeys and ancient city centres. The appetite is catered for too, with a wide variety of local foods accompanied by good-quality wine. In summary, the Camino has something for everyone. *¡Buen Camino!* (have a good journey).

HISTORY

The earliest known inhabitants of northern Spain (from around 800,000BC) were pre-hominids and Neanderthals, whose remains have been discovered at Atapuerca near Burgos (Stage 7). Later, successive waves of Stone Age, Bronze Age and Iron Age civilisations arrived from Central Asia via western Europe. The last of these were Indo-European speaking Celtic tribes who arrived in Spain during the sixth century BC.

Roman civilisation (218BC–AD439)
The Romans came to Spain in 218BC, initially to conquer the Carthaginians who had settled along the Mediterranean coast. From here Roman control spread slowly north and west in campaigns against Celtic tribes but it was not until 19BC that all of Iberia came under Roman rule. The Romans involved local tribal leaders in government and control of the territory. With an improved standard of living, the conquered tribes soon became thoroughly romanised. Indeed, the Roman province of Hispania became an important part of the Roman Empire, with three emperors being born there: Trajan (ruled

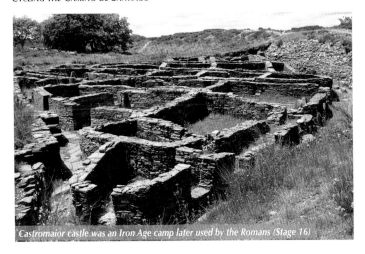

Castromaior castle was an Iron Age camp later used by the Romans (Stage 16)

AD98–117), Hadrian (AD117–38) and Marcus Aurelius (AD161–80). The VII legion was settled in Legio (León, Stage 11) while nearby gold mines made Asturica Augusta (Astorga, Stage 12) a rich and prosperous town. Roads were built linking cities across Iberia, including one across northern Spain, south of the Cantabrian mountains from Pompaelo (Pamplona, Stage 2) to Brigantum (near Coruña) via León and Astorga that 1000 years later would be partly followed by the Camino. The Romans knew this as Via Lactea (Milky Way) as it was said to follow the stars to Finis Terrae (the end of the world) on the Atlantic coast of Galicia.

During the fifth century AD, the Romans came under increasing pressure from Germanic tribes from the east who invaded Gaul (France) and moved on into Hispania. Roman rule ended in AD439 with the Romans allowing the Christian and partly romanised Visigoths to take control of most of Spain after a brief interlude of Suevi (Swabian) rule.

Visigoths (AD439–711)
Despite consolidating power by defeating other Germanic tribes and inheriting the well-established levers of Roman rule, Visigoth rulers did not have the same grip on power that their predecessors held. Internal disputes were common with periodic civil wars, assassinations, usurpations of power and free-roaming warlords all destabilising the state. Like other civilisations of the Dark Ages, the Visigoths left little in the way of architecture or art and few written documents, resulting in the soubriquet 'invisigoths'. After

AD585, when they conquered Galicia, they controlled all of Iberia apart from the Basque country, Asturias and Cantabria on the north coast.

Moorish invasion (AD711–22)

From AD618, when the prophet Mohamed fled from Mecca to Medina, Islam spread rapidly through the Middle East and along the north African coast, arriving in what is now Morocco by the end of the seventh century. In AD711, the Moorish army of the Umayyad Caliphate crossed the Strait of Gibraltar and invaded southern Spain where they defeated a Visigoth army at the Battle of Guadalete. King Roderic and many nobles were killed, leaving Spain with no army and no leadership. This allowed the Moors to capture much of the country unopposed.

The small independent kingdom of Asturias, on the north coast, became the focus of resistance to Moorish occupation. In AD722, a Moorish army confronted a small Asturian force led by Don Pelayo occupying a narrow gorge at Covadonga in the Cantabrian mountains. Here, against all odds, the Moors suffered their first defeat in Spain. This Asturian victory is regarded as the beginning of a Christian fightback against the Moors which became known as the Reconquista (Reconquest).

The Reconquista (AD722–1492)

Other victories followed with the boundaries of Asturias being extended slowly west into Galicia, east into Cantabria and south over the Cantabrian mountains into León. Christian legend tells of a victory at

San Juan de Ortega monastery church (Stage 7)

Clavijo (AD834) which played a major role in the development of the Camino. The apostle James, wielding a sword and riding a white horse, is said to have appeared at the head of the Christian army and led them to victory in his name. This vision became Santiago Matamoros (St James the Moor-slayer), an iconic figure portrayed all along the Camino and a rallying cry for soldiers in the Christian armies.

As the Reconquista pushed the Moors south, the cities of Pamplona, Burgos and León were freed from Moorish rule, becoming capitals of independent kingdoms in Navarre, Castile and León. The capital of Christian Spain moved south too, first from Oviedo to León, then to Valladolid and eventually to Madrid after the Moors were driven from central Spain in 1212. The Moors held on in Andalucía for nearly 300 years until 1492 when the fall of Granada ended 781 years of Muslim involvement in Spain.

Imperial Spain (1492–1807)

When Christopher Columbus, an Italian from Genoa employed by the Spanish crown, discovered land in the Caribbean in 1492, he unwittingly changed the economic fortune of Spain. Spanish colonisation of large parts of the New World led to discoveries of vast lodes of gold and silver which made Spain the richest country in Europe. On the death of Ferdinand II (1516), the Spanish crown passed to Charles V, a Habsburg who became

Holy Roman Emperor. During his reign and that of his son Phillip II, Spain entered a golden age controlling large parts of Europe with overseas colonies in the Americas, Africa and Asia. Unfortunately, with the exception of Burgos and León which sat on north–south trade routes, this prosperity was not shared along the Camino where the decline of the pilgrimage led to economic depression and falling populations.

After 1700, the Spanish crown passed to the Bourbons, the French royal house. For the next 100 years Spanish economic and political policies were closely connected with France. The empire survived until 1807, when French emperor Napoleon entered Spain intent on capturing Portugal and bringing it into his Continental System in order to isolate his greatest threat, Britain. The ensuing Peninsular War (1808–14) between Britain (defending its Portuguese ally), and France and Spain caused much devastation across Iberia. Lack of central government caused South American colonies to take control of their own affairs, which after the war led to unilateral declarations of independence throughout the New World.

Instability and civil wars (1814–1939)

Weakened by war and unable to maintain its empire, 19th-century Spain declined from the richest country in Europe to one of the poorest. Apart from development in the regional enclaves of Catalonia and the Basque country, Spain missed much of the Industrial Revolution that swept Europe. The country was politically unstable with numerous constitutions, three internal wars (the Carlist Wars of 1833–39 and 1872–76 and the Civil War of 1936–39), two abdications, two volatile republics, military coups, regional uprisings, bombings and assassinations. The Civil War, a vicious confrontation between right and left, regionalism and centralisation, clerical and secular power divided the country almost equally between supporters of an incipient republic and the nationalism of Generalísimo Francisco Franco. Most of the area passed through by the Camino was a conservative part of Spain that generally supported the nationalist cause. Indeed, Burgos (Stage 7) was Franco's headquarters during the conflict.

Modern-day Spain (post 1939)

Victory for the nationalists was followed by a long period of tightly controlled stability while the country recovered slowly from the trauma. When Franco died (1975), Spain reverted to a constitutional monarchy and reinstated a degree of regional autonomy. After joining the European Union in 1989, an influx of development funding led to a dramatic increase in economic activity with new motorways and railways criss-crossing the country, new airports and new factories. City centres have seen

major developments. Spain suffered in the financial crash of 2007 but is now recovering. The country was a founding member of the Euro zone, while the Shengen agreement allowing the free movement of people has resulted in open borders with France and Portugal.

THE CAMINO

Medieval Camino (AD813–1562)

St James was one of the 12 apostles of Jesus Christ. The bible (Acts 12:1–2) tells us that he was beheaded in Jerusalem, probably in AD44. Before he was killed, James had travelled to Spain to spread Christian teaching, although this does not appear in contemporary accounts. After his death his body was returned by boat to Spain where it was taken ashore at Padron in Galicia, carried inland and buried on a remote hillside.

Nearly 800 years later in AD813, a Galician shepherd was led by a star to discover the remains of a long-dead body buried in a field. He reported his find to the local bishop who identified the bones as the remains of St James. A church built over the grave was rebuilt many times, evolving into a great cathedral surrounded by the medieval city of Santiago de Compostela (St James of the Field of Stars). This discovery was a godsend for the leaders of the Reconquista who adopted James as the figurehead of their fight against the Moors and

The body of St James is kept in a casket in Santiago cathedral (Stage 18)

patron saint of Spain. A slow trickle of pilgrims, who believed that by touching the bones of St James they could gain absolution of their sins and thus ensure entry to heaven, began making their way to Santiago.

By AD900 the Moors had been driven from a long strip of land across northern Spain immediately south of the Cantabrian mountains. This territory became an uninhabited no-man's land with Christian Spaniards reluctant to repopulate the area due to fear of Moorish return. The transit of pilgrims, mostly from France crossing Spain on their way to Santiago, was encouraged by the Kings of Navarre and León as a way of promoting settlement. Spaniards moved in to service the pilgrims, while some of the pilgrims themselves, appreciating the opportunity to cultivate empty lands,

settled in the area on their way back from Santiago. Towns and cities grew up along the route with inns, hostels, churches and hospitals to serve the pilgrims and stone bridges enabling them to cross rivers.

For the following three centuries the number of pilgrims continued to grow. A significant boost came when King Alfonso VI of León and Castile (ruled 1065–1109) invited the reformed Benedictine monastery of Cluny in Burgundy to participate in the construction and management of monasteries and churches along the route. These were often built by French craftsmen in a distinctive French-influenced style. Chivalrous orders, including the Knights Templars who built a large castle at Ponferrada (Stage 13), were given duties to protect pilgrims. The first guide to the route, the Codex Calixtinus thought to be by the monk Aymeric Picaud, was written about 1140 and it is believed that by the end of the 12th century 250,000 pilgrims were making the journey annually. The numbers began declining in the 14th century after the Black Death (1346–53) swept through Europe killing nearly half the population and, although the pilgrimage remained popular, 13th-century levels of participation were not matched until the 21st century.

Decline of the Camino (1517–95)

Martin Luther, a German monk and professor of theology, published his 95 theses in 1517. These criticised many practices of the Catholic church including two elements central to the Camino: the idolisation of relics and granting of indulgences. Luther's teaching and that of contemporary theologians such as Erasmus, Knox and Calvin instigated a Protestant Reformation which took hold rapidly across northern and western Europe. This growth of Protestantism further reduced the number of pilgrims setting off for Santiago. In France the church became divided between Catholic devotees of the status quo and Protestant Huguenots who supported the Reformation. A series of devastating religious wars broke out starting in 1562, culminating in 1595 with holy war between France and Spain where the inquisition ensured the continuing supremacy of Catholic teaching. International pilgrim travel became difficult and dangerous; by the end of the 16th century the medieval pilgrimage was over.

Modern Camino

For three centuries few pilgrims made the journey to Santiago. Pilgrim infrastructure along the Camino fell into disuse and ruin. In 1884 Pope Leo XIII declared that the bones at Santiago were indeed those of St James, but this did little to re-awake interest in the pilgrimage. Two world wars and the Spanish Civil War continued to make the journey difficult and unappealing. Post-Second World War interest was fuelled by the publication in 1957

Dr Elías Valiña Sampedro, who was the priest at O Cebreiro (Stage 14), waymarked the Camino by painting yellow arrows

of *The Road to Santiago* by Anglo-Irish academic Walter Starkey, which brought the Camino to an English-speaking audience.

The most significant element in the revival of the Camino was the work of Dr Elías Valiña Sampedro, an academic from Salamanca University who was also parish priest at O Cebreiro (Stage 14). He wrote his thesis on the medieval pilgrimage and in 1984 took a pot of paint and started marking the route with the yellow arrow waymarks that have now become synonymous with the Camino. He persuaded local parishes to re-open long-closed pilgrim albergues and local government to improve track surfaces and divert the route away from busy roads, work

which has continued since his death in 1989. The route you will follow is very much Dr Sampedro's legacy. Do take a few minutes to visit his monument beside O Cebreiro church and thank him for his efforts.

Coverage in popular culture is now widespread, including *The Way* (2010), a film written and directed by Emilio Estevez and starring Martin Sheen. This and much other publicity has dramatically increased the number of peregrinos reaching Santiago from under 1000 in 1985, to 55,000 in 2000, and over 325,000 (20,000 of whom were cyclists) in 2017. The Pilgrim Reception Office in Santiago (https://oficinadelperegrino.com) publishes daily statistics showing pilgrim arrivals, detailed by nationality, mode

Santiago Matamoros, the aggressive image of Santiago the Moor-slayer, Burgos cathedral (Stage 7)

of transport, start point of the pilgrimage and motivation. These show that approximately 180,000 pilgrims used the Camino Francés with 50,000 travelling the whole route either passing through St Jean-Pied-de-Port or starting in Navarre. Other popular starting points are León, Ponferrada and O Cebreiro. However, the most popular of all is Sarria (Stage 15), 113km from Santiago. The 80,000 walkers who start here are attracted by a provision in the rules for awarding the Compostela certificate for completing the route (the present-day equivalent of a medieval absolution). This provides that certificates will be given to walkers who complete 100km to Santiago and Sarria is the first place outside this distance that can be reached by public transport. Cyclists and horse-riders are required to travel 200km in order to qualify for a Compostela, giving a start point in Ponferrada (Stage 13).

In 1178, Pope Alexander III introduced the concept of Jubilee Years for St James, years when the saint's day (25 July) falls on a Sunday. In these years the Door of Pardon at the rear of Santiago cathedral is open and pilgrims who pass through it earn pardon for their sins. During the medieval Camino, a few other churches along the route were granted the same privilege, thus allowing sick and dying pilgrims who could not reach Santiago to obtain pardon. Jubilee Years are popular times to undertake the pilgrimage and in 2010 more than 100,000 extra

pilgrims travelled the Camino. Similar increases are anticipated in future Jubilee Years (2027 and 2032).

Throughout the Camino you will encounter many statues and representations of St James. These fall into two sharply contrasting groups. The peaceful side of James bringing the gospel to Spain is represented by Santiago Peregrino in the form of a cloaked pilgrim with a wooden staff and often wearing a scallop shell. By contrast, Santiago Matamoros is a mounted figure on a horse using a lance or sword to kill Moors, representing the warrior James leading the fight for Christianity.

THE ROUTES

When Dr Sampedro started marking a route for the modern Camino, he tried to identify and follow the way used by medieval pilgrims. This caused many problems. Long stretches had become asphalt surfaced roads, requiring peregrinos to walk along the side of often busy highways. As numbers grew, regional and provincial councils addressed this problem by either providing *sendas* (gravel trails parallel with the road) or diverting the route onto tracks through neighbouring fields. Today these trails and tracks form the backbone of the Camino followed by walking pilgrims. They are classified as bridleways and are legally accessible by horse riders and cyclists in addition to pedestrians. This route, which is best suited for mountain bikes, provides the basis for the main route in this guide, although there are a few places where a combination of steep gradient and rough track conditions make it necessary for cyclists to deviate slightly from the walked Camino.

The roads, which the modern Camino has moved away from, provide the base for an alternative road route, which apart from one short stretch is entirely asphalt surfaced. These two routes are fully described in this guide where the Camino for mountain bikes based on the walkers' route is referred to as the 'camino route' and the road alternative is called the 'road route'. There are many shared stretches and, on every stage, both routes start and finish at the same point.

From St Jean-Pied-de-Port on the French side of the Pyrenees, Stage 1 climbs up and over the mountains using one of the lowest Pyrenean passes to reach Roncesvalles abbey in Spain, a place with historic connections going back to Roland in AD778. Descent on Stage 2 into the Arga valley takes the route to Pamplona in Navarre, a partly Basque-speaking city famous for the annual running of the bulls. Continuing across Navarre (Stages 3–4), the Camino climbs over a windswept ridge then passes through the ancient religious centre of Estella before reaching the wine-producing city of Logroño in the Rioja region. Stage 5 passes close to some of the highest quality vineyards in Spain, while Stages 6–7 climb steadily up and over the forested Montes

de Oca and bare limestone Sierra de Atapuerca before descending into El Cid's city of Burgos.

Between Burgos and León (Stages 8–11) the route crosses the northern tip of the meseta, a vast area of rolling high-level chalk downland that occupies much of central Spain. This was a difficult area for medieval pilgrims, with long distances between villages, very little water and no shade which still offers a challenge today. The small towns and villages passed through are undergoing an economic revival brought by the modern Camino after 400 years of stagnation and population decline. León, just beyond the mid-point of the journey, is a popular place for a short break from cycling. This former Roman city and early capital of medieval Spain has outstanding buildings representing 900 years of architectural development from a Romanesque basilica that holds a mausoleum of former monarchs, through to a French-Gothic cathedral and a Renaissance former monastery that is nowadays the most ornate Spanish *parador* (luxury hotel) to a modernist Gaudí-designed private palace (Appendix G contains a brief summary of Spanish architectural styles).

Stage 12 runs through the Páramo, a fertile area irrigated by water from the Cantabrian mountains, to Astorga, a former Roman town that prospered from nearby gold mines. Stage 13 climbs into the Maragatería and over the forested Montes de León,

The Camino crosses the meseta, an area of high-level downland with little shade (Stages 8–12)

part of the Cantabrian mountains, then descends steeply to the Knights Templar town of Ponferrada. Stage 14 crosses the fertile Bierzo basin then climbs steeply to reach O Cebreiro perched high in the mountains on the edge of Galicia. The final four stages (Stages 15–18) pass through rolling Galician green hills and valleys. The Camino ends at Santiago de Compostela, a city of monasteries, churches and ancient streets surrounding the pilgrims' ultimate destination, the tomb of St James housed inside a great 11th-century cathedral.

NATURAL ENVIRONMENT

Physical geography

The north-eastern border of Spain is formed by the Pyrenees mountains. Composed of a core of granite covered by limestone outer flanks, the range was pushed up by a collision between the Iberian and European tectonic plates approximately 50 million years ago. South of the Pyrenees is the Ebro basin. Originally connected to the Bay of Biscay, this basin was raised by the plate collision then filled with sands, gravels and clays brought down from the mountains by riverine erosion.

The centre of Spain is a high chalk plateau of rolling downland, known as the meseta (tableland) which covers much of the region of Castile y León. This is an area of large arable farms typically growing wheat and sunflowers, with a few small villages, little groundwater and no shade. The Camino (Stages 8–12) crosses the northern part of this plateau. Modern irrigation schemes bringing water down from the Cantabrian mountains have enhanced the agricultural fertility of the western meseta.

Flanking the northern edge of the meseta, the limestone Cantabrian mountains run east–west parallel with the Bay of Biscay. For much of the route they can be seen on the northern horizon until Stage 13 when the route climbs over a subsidiary range known as the Montes de León. The Bierzo basin, between the Montes de León and the Galician massif, is a highly fertile area of sedimentary deposits with an attractive microclimate where vines, fruit and vegetables are grown. The last four stages (14–18) run through the Galician massif, an area of low rounded granite mountains and hills, originally heavily forested but now a mixture of woods and pastoral farms.

Wildlife

While several small mammals and reptiles (including rabbits, hares, squirrels and snakes) may be encountered scuttling across the track, and deer seen in forests and fields, this is not a route where you will encounter unusual wildlife. There are bears and wolves in the remote parts of the Cantabrian mountains, but not near the Camino.

PREPARATION

When to go

The routes can be cycled at any time of year, although they are best followed between April and October

Storks' nests on the church bell tower at Puente del Castro (Stage 11)

when the days are longer, the weather is warmer and there is no chance of snow. July and August are very hot and very busy, with spring and autumn the most pleasant times to make the journey.

How long will it take?

Both routes have been broken into 18 stages averaging approximately 43km per stage. A fit cyclist, cycling an average of 80km per day using roads or 55km per day off-road should be able to complete the road route in 10 days and the camino route in two weeks. A faster cyclist averaging 100km per day could complete the road route in eight days. There are many places to stay along both routes making it possible to tailor daily distances to your requirements. When planning your schedule, allow at least a day in Santiago at the end of your pilgrimage to obtain your Compostela and visit the cathedral. If you want a mid-journey break, León is an attractive city with many things to see.

What kind of cycle is suitable?

The camino route mostly follows well-surfaced gravel tracks with frequent undulations, although there are a few rough stages. This is best cycled on a mountain bike or a gravel bike (a simplified mountain bike designed for both gravel trails and roads) with a wide range of gears (typically a rear cassette with 11–36 teeth and front chainrings of 26/36/48 teeth), off-road tyres and disc brakes. Front suspension is beneficial as it absorbs much of the vibration. It is passable on a hybrid (a lightweight but strong cross between a touring cycle and a mountain bike) provided this is set up with low gearing and off-road tyres.

Apart from two short sections of gravel surface on Stage 5 between Logroño and Santo Domingo de la Calzada, the road route uses asphalt surfaced roads throughout. It is cyclable on all types of road cycle (hybrid, tourer, racing bike) provided panniers can be fitted. If you use a mountain bike or cross-trail for the road route it should be set up with road tyres and have the suspension locked out.

Straight handlebars, with bar-ends enabling you to vary your position regularly, are recommended. Make sure your cycle is serviced and lubricated before you start, particularly the brakes, gears and chain. Your choice of tyres is as important as the cycle. For the camino route you should use knobbly off-road tyres. However, these are not suitable for the road route where you need a good-quality touring tyre with a deeper tread and a slightly wider profile than you would use for everyday cycling at home. To reduce the chance of punctures, choose tyres with puncture resistant armouring, such as a Kevlar™ band.

Bicycle rental and bag transfer

An alternative to taking your own bicycle is to rent one to collect when you arrive. Hire companies in Pamplona, Burgos and Santiago can deliver a cycle to your start point and collect it after your journey. Most offer good-quality bikes with back-up repair coverage. Many walkers use bag transfer services and these can be used by cyclists to complete the Camino without panniers.

PILGRIM CREDENTIALS AND INFORMATION

To stay in albergues, obtain discounted entry to many monuments along the route and most importantly obtain your Compostela in Santiago, you will need pilgrim credentials also known as a pilgrim passport. National Camino organisations, including the Confraternity of St James in Britain (www.csj.org.uk), issue credentials and provide advice for pilgrims. Other national confraternities are listed in

Appendix D. If you leave home without a credential, you can pick one up at the Pilgrim Information Office in St Jean-Pied-de-Port or at Roncesvalles abbey. Credentials are available to all self-propelled peregrinos (walkers, cyclists and horse riders but not motorists or motor-bikers) irrespective of religious faith.

As you travel along the route, the credential should be stamped with an official stamp and dated at least once a day (twice a day for cyclists who start in Ponferrada). These stamps can be obtained from albergues, hotels, town halls, tourist offices, churches and cathedrals and even some restaurants. Upon arrival in Santiago, the stamped credential should be presented to the Pilgrim Reception Office (33 Rúa das Carretas, Santiago 15705, open 0800–2100) where it will be

Pilgrim credentials need to be stamped every day to qualify for a Compostela

inspected and your Compostela issued. This is a certificate showing you completed the Camino and is the modern-day successor to the medieval indulgence although it no longer offers to pardon your sins or grant entry to heaven. Beware, long queues often form at the office and it can take several hours before you are seen.

GETTING THERE AND BACK

Getting to the start
St Jean-Pied-de-Port is the terminus of a local railway line from Bayonne, served by four trains per day that carry cycles and take about one hour to reach St Jean. From London, St Jean can be reached in a day either by flying to Biarritz then cycling to Bayonne and continuing by train, or by travelling by train throughout.

Eurostar trains from London St Pancras to Paris Gare du Nord carry cycles as do some (but not all) of the TGV trains from Paris Gare Montparnasse to Bayonne. If you leave London by 08.00, cycle across Paris

from station to station (6km) to catch a TGV from Montparnasse before 13.00, you will arrive in Bayonne in time to connect with the last train to St Jean arriving about 19.00. If you leave London on a later train you will need to overnight in Bayonne and catch the first train next morning, arriving in St Jean before 09.00.

Eurostar trains from London, that take under two and a half hours to reach Paris via the Channel tunnel, carry up to six cycles per train: two fully assembled plus four dismantled bikes packed in specially designed fibreglass bike boxes provided by Eurostar. Bookings, which open six months in advance, must be made through EuroDespatch at St Pancras (tel +44 (0)344 822 5822). Prices vary from £30–£55 depending on how far ahead you book and whether your cycle is dismantled or fully assembled. Cycles must be checked in at the EuroDespatch centre beside the bus drop-off point at the back of St Pancras station, at least 60 minutes before departure. If you need to dismantle your bike, Eurodespatch will provide

GETTING FROM BIARRITZ AIRPORT TO BAYONNE STATION

Follow exit road from Biarritz airport and turn R at roundabout onto main road (Ave d'Espagne, D810). Continue ahead for 4.5km, going over three more roundabouts. At fourth roundabout, turn L (third exit, Allées Paulmy, sp Centre-Ville). At end, bear R following one-way system (Ave Léon Bonnat), passing public gardens L. Turn L on bridge over river Nive and continue ahead on second bridge over river Adour. Bear L to reach roundabout in front of Bayonne station (7.5km).

CROSSING PARIS: GARE DU NORD TO GARE MONTPARNASSE

After arrival in Paris you need to cycle through the heart of Paris from Gare du Nord to Gare Montparnasse using a mixture of dedicated cycle tracks beside wide boulevards, marked cycle lanes and contra-flow cycling along one-way streets. Go ahead opposite main entrance to Gare du Nord along Bvd de Denain (one-way street with contra-flow cycling permitted). At end turn half L (Bvd de Magenta, cycle track R) and follow this SE. Turn R just before number 77 (Rue de Faubourg St Denis) and continue straight ahead doglegging R and L past Porte St Denis archway into Rue St Denis. Where this becomes one-way with contra-flow cycling continue ahead for 1.25km to reach major crossroads beside number 12. Turn R (Rue de Rivoli) then first L (Rue de Lavandières Ste Opportune) and continue ahead to reach T-junction on banks of river Seine. Turn L (Quai de la Mégisserie) and R over river on Pont au Change bridge (3km).

Continue over second bridge (Pont St Michel) and fork R (Place St Michel, becoming Rue Danton). Cross Bvd St Germain and turn R beside road. Soon turn L (Rue de l'Odéon) and fork R (Rue de Condé). Turn second R (Rue St Sulpice) and continue ahead past St Sulpice church and square with fountain (both L) into Rue du Vieux Colombier. Turn L (Rue de Rennes) at traffic lights and continue for 1km. Bear R beside Tour Montparnasse L to reach Gare Montparnasse L (6km).

tools and packing advice. Leave yourself plenty of time for dismantling and packing. In Paris Gare du Nord, cycles can be collected from Geoparts baggage office which can be reached by a path L of platform 3. More information at www.eurostar.com.

From Paris Gare Montparnasse, there are TGV high-speed trains approximately every two hours to Bayonne. Most of these carry up to four cycles which must be booked in advance at the same time as booking your passenger ticket. Cyclists travel with their cycles in a dedicated second-class compartment at one end of the train. Bookings are made through SNCF, www.oui.sncf.com.

Intermediate access

There are airports at Pamplona (Stage 2), Logroño (Stage 4), Burgos (Stage 7) and Léon (Stage 11) but none of these has direct flights to the UK; a connecting flight is necessary through Madrid, Barcelona or Frankfurt.

These four cities also have railway stations and there are other stations at Frómista (Stage 9), Sahagún (Stage 10), Astorga (Stage 12), Ponferrada (Stage 13) and Sarria (Stage 15). The only part where a railway parallels

Houses in St Jean-Pied-de-Port overlooking the river Nive (Stage 1)

the Camino is between Sahagún and Astorga via Léon (Stages 11–12). In Spain neither AVE high-speed trains nor regular long-distance trains carry bicycles, although medium distance and regional trains do have bike spaces. Cycle carriage is free on these trains, but you must reserve a space before you travel.

Getting home

The easiest way to return home from Santiago to the UK with your cycle is by plane. Santiago airport, 12km from the city centre and passed on Stage 18, has regular flights to many European cities. La Coruña airport, one hour from Santiago by hourly trains which carry cycles, also has flights to various airports. Airlines have different requirements regarding how cycles are presented and some,

but not all, make a charge which you should pay when booking as it is usually greater at the airport. All require tyres partially deflated, handlebars turned and pedals removed (loosen pedals beforehand to make them easier to remove at the airport). Most will accept your cycle in a transparent polythene bike bag, however, some insist on the use of a cardboard bike box.

In Santiago, Velocípedo bicicletas (Rúa de San Pedro 23, tel +34 981 580 260, www.elvelocipedo.com) can supply bike boxes and offer a packing service (€21 or €45 including taxi to airport). An unusual but reliable way to get your cycle home is by post using the Spanish *correos* (post office) Paq Bicicleta service. They have two offices in Santiago – the central post office, Rúa do Franco 4, or a branch inside the Pilgrims' Reception

Office (Rúa das Carretas 33) – who will organise packing and despatch your bike to any overseas address. Cost to the UK is €90. This may seem expensive, but with airlines charging up to €70 to carry a cycle, plus the cost of the bike box and airport taxi, it can be cheaper than flying it home yourself. Should you not complete the whole route, they can deliver your cycle home from most intermediate towns on the Camino.

You can return home by train, but it is a complicated three-day journey. Neither the one daily direct train from Santiago to Irun on the French border, nor the AVE high-speed trains that link Santiago with Madrid via Valladolid and Madrid with Paris, carry cycles. The only route possible is to catch a RENFE regional train to La Coruña and a local train to Ferrol. From there FEVE narrow gauge trains run along the north coast of Spain. These slow trains stopping at all stations take two days to reach Bilbao, requiring an overnight stop in either Oviedo or Santander (there are pilgrim albergues in both cities). From Bilbao, Euskotren services run via San Sebastián to Irun for another overnight stop. From Irun you can catch an SNCF TGV train to Paris and Eurostar to London.

There are two alternatives to travelling all the way by train. One is to use FEVE to reach Santander or Bilbao then catch a ferry across the Bay of Biscay to Britain or Ireland. Brittany Ferries (www.brittany-ferries.

co.uk) operate six sailings per week between Spain and Plymouth or Portsmouth in southern England with two per week to Cork in the Republic of Ireland. The second is to travel by Alsa bus (www.alsa.es) from Santiago to Bilbao then continue either by ferry to Portsmouth or by train via San Sebastián and Irun as described above. There are two buses per day (one daytime, one overnight) taking between 9 and 12 hours depending upon the route, carrying up to four cycles per departure. Alsa has a ticket agent inside the Santiago pilgrim reception office.

NAVIGATION

Waymarking

The camino route is fully waymarked throughout with yellow arrows, scallop shells, waymarks, stone pillars and Camino signposts. These waymarks are so frequent that if you travel for more than 500 metres without seeing a waymark of some kind, you have almost certainly taken a wrong turn and need to go back.

The road route is less frequently waymarked and where signs do occur they are often placed in the middle of long stretches of straight road, acting more as a confirmation that you are on the correct route rather than an indication of which route to follow. In some places white arrows painted on the road show directions for cyclists. While useful, these are

The Camino is waymarked with a variety of symbols, mostly in yellow or blue

inconsistent and cannot be relied upon. In general, the road route follows four Spanish national roads: N-135, N-111, N-120 and N-547. In some regions, where motorways have taken traffic off these main roads, they have been reclassified as regional roads and renumbered accordingly. This is particularly the case in Navarre, where the N-111 has been renumbered NA-1110, reverting to N-111 when it reaches Logroño.

Maps

It is possible to cycle both routes using only the maps in this book, particularly the camino route which is waymarked throughout. If you want a series of maps at a larger scale and that show a wider area than that covered by the strip maps, IGN España (the Spanish equivalent of the Ordnance Survey) produce a boxed set of 11 sheet maps at 1:50,000 while Michelin publish a map booklet at 1:150,000 (map 160). Camino Guides publish a map booklet that has hand drawn maps of varying scale (each stage is drawn to fit one page with scales differing from map to map and most confusingly between parts of the same map), and while these maps are not particularly accurate nor all embracing, the booklet does show the location of, and give details about, all accommodation opportunities en-route.

ACCOMMODATION

For the whole route there are a wide variety of places to stay overnight. The stage descriptions identify places known to have accommodation, but new properties open every year so the list is by no means exhaustive. An updated list of albergues and other accommodation for the whole Camino can be obtained from Les Amis du Chemin de St Jacques office in St Jean-Pied-de-Port and the Confraternity of St James in London also produces an annual pilgrim guide with up-to-date accommodation listings plus an occasional cycling supplement intended for use with its guide. Tourist information offices can provide lists of local accommodation in all categories but unlike in northern Europe do not provide a booking service. Booking ahead is seldom necessary, except in high season (July and August). The search engine www.booking.com has the widest range of accommodation in northern Spain. Most properties are cycle friendly and will find you a secure overnight place for your pride and joy. Prices for all kinds of accommodation are lower than in the UK.

Albergues and youth hostels

Albergues (marked with a white A on a blue sign on the outside of the building) are the most numerous and popular type of accommodation along the

Les Amis du Chemin de St Jacques office issues pilgrim credentials (Stage 1)

Albergue Gaucelmo in Rabanal del Camino is run by British volunteers from the Confraternity of St James (Stage 13)

Camino and are a good place to stay if you want to meet and converse with other pilgrims. Albergues are everywhere, even tiny hamlets may have two or more. Many new ones have opened in recent years, some too new to appear on accommodation lists. There are three kinds: municipal (run by the local government), religious (run by churches, monasteries and other religious organisations) and private. The average price is between €7–€12 for a dormitory bed in a municipal or religious albergue, slightly higher for private albergues which often have individual rooms as well as dormitories. However, the large number of new albergues opened in recent years provide intense competition, which is keeping prices down. Some religious albergues have no quoted price and ask instead for donations. As a guide, you should donate the same as you would pay for a municipal albergue. There are 11 hostelling international youth hostels, but four are in or around Pamplona and so they are not well spread. In practice, youth hostels are similar to albergues.

Albergues usually close during the day, opening around 1600. In high season (July and August) some busy municipal and religious refuges give preference to walkers and may not accept cyclists until after 1800. Lights out is at 2200, with many walking pilgrims rising before 0600 for an early start. Blankets are usually provided; all you need is a sleeping sheet and a towel. Many albergues have a *cocina* (kitchen) where you can prepare your own food, while some have a *comedor* (dining room) that serves a *menú peregrino*, a cheap fixed price meal. Almost all will provide a secure place to store your cycle.

Hoteles, hostales, pensiones and casas rurales

These establishments provide accommodation in separate rooms, usually with private toilet and shower but sometimes cheaper hostels and pensions have shared facilities. Hotels (marked with a white H on a blue sign) vary from five-star properties to modest local establishments. At the top end there are five paradores, state-owned luxury hotels in restored historic buildings. Hostales (marked with white Hs on a blue sign) are smaller hotels and guest houses with fewer services. Most hotels and hostels offer a full meal service. Pensions (marked with a white P on a blue sign) provide simple accommodation, often using rooms in apartment buildings. A *casa rural* is a country guest house usually offering B&B and evening meals to guests.

Camping

Economic accommodation in albergues is so widely available that very few people choose to camp. Most campsites are aimed at longer stay holiday makers rather than overnighting pilgrims.

Where to eat

There are many places where peregrinos can eat and drink, varying from snack bars to Michelin-starred restaurants. English language menus are widely available along the Camino either printed or on chalkboards. Eating out in Spain is not expensive and almost every village will have at least one small restaurant offering a *menú peregrino* (set-price pilgrim meal including wine) at around €10, usually with long opening hours to suit walking peregrinos.

Local restaurants (*comedores*), frequented by working people rather than peregrinos, are often attached to bars or local inns. They are sometimes hard to spot, being just a door at the back of the bar that is only open at Spanish mealtimes (1400–1500, 2100–2300). Historically they had to offer a cheap filling *menú del día* (lunchtime set-price meal) consisting of three courses and a half bottle of wine, affordable to working men. Prices for the menú del día are similar to pilgrim meal prices but there will probably be only an a la carte menu in the evenings. If you are going to eat a la carte, you need to request *la carta*, asking for the menu will get you the set-price meal. Roadside restaurants (*ventas*) offer similarly priced food aimed at truck drivers and passing motorists. Cafeterias, mostly in towns and cities, generally offer *platos combinados* (single course, drinks not included) rather than a menú del día. These tend to be blander options (fish and chips, ham and eggs, etc) of a pan-European nature, but with similar prices.

Full service restaurants, sometimes attached to hotels, offer à la carte menus. They have a grading system (one–five forks) reflecting the price, variety and quality of food served.

If you want a series of quick snacks rather than a full meal, tapas bars provide a wide range of choice. In the larger cities (Pamplona, Logroño, Burgos, León, Santiago) large numbers of tapas bars are concentrated in a small area making an evening *paseo* (walk) from bar to bar trying different tapas an attractive alternative to sitting down to a restaurant set meal. Single portions (*pinchos*) and

small filled bread rolls (*bocadillos*) are usually displayed on the bar counter while larger portions (*raciones*) can be ordered from the barman.

During the summer season, pop-up bars and restaurants spring up along the route. These serve food and drink from caravans, marquees, vans or basic wooden shelters; usually in the same place each year. They are often located where there are long distances between conventional refreshment providers such as the 12km stretch through the forested Montes de Oca between Villafranca Montes de Oca and San Juan de Ortega (Stage 7).

When to eat

Traditional Spanish eating hours differ significantly from the rest of Europe. Breakfast (*desayuno*), usually nothing more than coffee and a croissant, is

Tapas bars in all the major cities offer a wide variety of tapas

taken about 0900. Lunch (*almuerzo*) is late, usually between 1400–1500 while dinner (*cena*) is even later, between 2100–2300. Light snacks are consumed mid-morning while more substantial snacks, such as tapas, are taken in early evening.

This pattern of eating is not really suitable for pilgrims, who like to start early (often before 0700) and go to bed by 2200. Restaurants catering to pilgrims reflect this by offering early breakfasts, lunch between 1200–1400 and dinner from 1900 with a *menú peregrino* offered at both lunchtime and early evening. Full a la carte dinners are usually served after 2100.

What to eat
Spanish cooking is generally Mediterranean in style with ample use of olive oil, garlic, tomatoes and other Mediterranean vegetables. While there are a number of regional specialities that you will encounter, much of the food offered in pilgrim menus is unadventurous and pan-Iberian in style. Most meals will start with soup, such as vegetable, *ajo* (garlic) or barley, or pasta. The most common main courses are *chuletas de cerdo* (pork chops) or *pollo* (chicken) followed by *postre* (dessert) of fruit, *flan* (cream caramel) or *arroz con leche* (rice pudding). Although it originated on the Mediterranean coast, *paella*, a dish of saffron rice, chicken and seafood, is widely available along the route. Other pan-Iberian dishes include *tortilla Española* (a thick omelette of eggs,

potatoes and onions, cut into sections and often served cold as a *bocadillo* filling), *jamón serrano* (cured ham) and *chorizos* (spicy sausages).

Regional cuisine consists mainly of hearty dishes using local ingredients. Navarre is known for *cordero* (lamb), *trucha con jamón* (trout wrapped in ham) and *menestra de verduras* (vegetable stew), while in La Rioja look out for *patatas a la Riojana* (potatoes roasted with chorizo and red peppers). In León you will find *morcilla* (black pudding/blood sausage) while *fabada* (bean and pork casserole), which originates from nearby Asturias, is widely available. Galician dishes include *caldo Gallego* (turnip top, potato and pork stew) and a wide range of *empanadas* (savoury pies made with meat or tuna). However, the main emphasis of food in Galicia centres around *vaca/ternera* (beef/veal) and dairy products in the hills and mountains and *pescado* (fish) and *mariscos* (seafood) nearer the coast. The biggest selling fish are *merluza* (hake), *bacalao* (cod), *salmón* and *dorada* (bream). Among a wide selection of seafood, the most common are *gambas* (prawns), *calamar* (squid) and *pulpo* (octopus): Melide (Stage 17) is famed for its octopus. *Vieiras a la Gallega* (scallops cooked with ham, onions and tomato sauce) are served in a scallop shell, the symbol of the Camino. They provide a fitting final meal for your journey, especially when accompanied by albariño white wine from the nearby Rias Baixas and finished off with a slice of *tarta Santiago* (almond tart decorated with another Camino symbol, the Santiago cross, etched into its dusting of sugar).

To finish the meal there are a wide variety of cheeses. Manchego, Spain's biggest selling cheese, is ubiquitous but there are also local cheeses to try. Cabrales (made from goats' milk blended with sheep and cows' milk) comes from Asturias while Roncal is a smoked sheep milk cheese from Navarre. Galicia is dairy country, producing Ulloa (flat) and Tetilla (breast shaped), both soft cows' milk cheese. Other Galician cows' milk cheese includes Cebreiro (hard, mild) and San Simón (smoked, orange coloured, conical).

What to drink

Viticulture was re-introduced to northern Spain by the French after the Moors had been expelled and the country has been a *vino* (wine) drinking country ever since. Well-bodied *vino de mesa tinto* (red table wine) is the staple tipple of most Spaniards, although *blanco* (white), *rosado* (rosé), *espumoso* (sparkling) and fortified wines are also available. In recent years there has been a move away from heavy red wines to lighter varieties. Table wine is automatically included in set menus (including pilgrim menus), usually a half bottle or 250mm carafe per person. Do not worry if you do not drink wine, *agua sin gas* (still water) or *agua con gas* (sparkling water) are available as alternatives but as a bottle of water is about the same price as a cheap bottle of wine you will not get a discount.

The Camino passes through the country's most renowned vineyard

Galicia is a land of rolling green hills with a mix of dairy farms and forest (Stages 15–18)

region in Rioja and neighbouring Navarre and other less well-known regions in León, the Bierzo and Galicia. In Rioja (Stage 5), tempranillo and garnacha grapes are used to produce mostly high-quality red wine, although production of white Rioja using viura and malvasía grapes is small but increasing. Vineyards around León (Stage 11) produce predominately red table wines while the Bierzo (Stage 14) produces softer red wine using mencía grapes and white wine with godello grapes. The cooler damper climate of Galicia (Stage 18) is suited to lighter wines than the rest of Spain, producing white wine from albariño grapes and some soft reds.

Consumption of *cerveza* (beer) is growing with sales doubling between 1976–2006. Light pils-style lagers predominate, mostly produced by multi-national brewers Heineken/Amstel/Cruzcampo and Carlsberg/Mahou/San Miguel and national brewer Estrella Damm. Two strengths are widely available, *cerveza clásica* (4.6 per cent alcohol) and *cerveza especial* (5.5 per cent). If you ask for a *cerveza*, you will usually be served bottled beer, if you want draught beer you need to order *una caña*. This is normally served in 200ml glasses, for a larger glass (400ml) ask for *caña grande*. In Navarre a *caña grande* is often called *una pinta* while in Galicia it is known as *uno bock*. *Cidra* (apple cider) is produced in northern Spain, mostly in Asturias. This is stronger than beer and so dry it will pucker your lips. Often served from casks, it is poured from height into small glasses in order to generate a slight spritz.

Since Spain joined the EU a lot of capital has been spent improving the quality of rural water supplies and connecting properties to mains water. As a result, tap water along the Camino is safe to drink and there is no health reason to purchase bottled water. There are many drinking water fountains along the route; most towns and villages have at least one and there are some in rural locations. These are tested by health authorities and marked whether or not they are safe to drink (*agua no potable* is not safe to drink!).

All the usual soft drinks (colas, lemonade, fruit juices, mineral waters) are widely available.

AMENITIES AND SERVICES

Grocery shops

All cities, towns and larger villages passed through have grocery stores, often supermarkets, and most have pharmacies. Most villages have a *panadería* (bakery) that bakes fresh bread every day. Local shops typically open on Mondays to Saturdays 09.30–13.30 and 16.30–20.00, while larger stores, supermarkets and department stores are generally open 10.00–21.00, but there are local variations. Most shops are closed on Sundays.

The steep track up to Alto del Perdón with Pamplona in the distance (Stage 3)

Cycle shops

Most towns have cycle shops with repair facilities equipped to repair and service all types of bike. Many will adjust brakes and gears, lubricate your chain and make minor repairs while you wait. Locations of cycle shops are shown in stage descriptions with full addresses listed in Appendix C, although this list is not exhaustive. Bicigrino is an association of cycle shops along the Camino that offer emergency repair services to peregrinos.

Currency and banks

Spain switched from Spanish pesetas to euros in 2002. Almost every town has a bank and most have ATM machines which enable you to make transactions in English. However very few offer over-the-counter currency exchange and the only way to obtain currency is to use ATM machines to withdraw cash from your personal account or from a prepaid travel card. Contact your bank to activate your bank card for use in Europe or put cash on a travel card. Credit or debit cards can be used for most purchases, although albergues generally accept cash only. Travellers' cheques are rarely used.

Telephone and internet

The whole route has mobile phone coverage. Contact your network provider to ensure your phone is enabled for foreign use with the optimum price package. International dialling codes are +44 for UK, +34 for Spain and +33 for France.

Almost all hotels, hostels, albergues and many restaurants make internet access available to guests, usually free of charge.

Electricity
Voltage is 220v, 50HzAC. Spain uses standard European twin round-pin plugs.

WHAT TO TAKE

Clothing and personal items
The route is undulating with a few steep climbs, consequently weight should be kept to a minimum. You will need clothes for cycling (shoes, socks, shorts/trousers, shirt, fleece, waterproofs) and clothes for evenings and days off. The best maxim is two of each, 'one to wear, one to wash'. Time of year makes a difference as you need more and warmer clothing in April/May and September/October when gloves and a woolly hat are needed for cold morning starts. A sun hat and sunglasses are essential. All of this clothing should be able to be washed en route, and a small tube or bottle of travel wash is useful.

In addition to your usual toiletries you will need sun cream and lip salve. You should take a simple first-aid kit. If staying in albergues, you will need a towel and torch (your cycle light should suffice).

One piece of decoration you may wish to attach to your panniers is a scallop shell. Medieval pilgrims brought such shells back from Santiago as 'proof' they had completed the journey. Modern peregrinos obtain such emblems early in their journey, often in St Jean-Pied-de-Port, and display them as a badge showing they are traversing the Camino.

A fully loaded cycle at the start of the Camino in St Jean-Pied-de-Port (Stage 1)

Cycle equipment

Everything you take needs to be carried on your cycle. Unless camping, a pair of rear panniers should be sufficient to carry all your clothing and equipment, although if camping, you may also need front panniers. Panniers should be 100 per cent watertight. If in doubt, pack everything inside a strong polythene lining bag. Rubble bags, obtainable from builders' merchants, are ideal for this purpose. A bar-bag is a useful way of carrying items you need to access quickly such as maps, sunglasses, camera, spare tubes, puncture kit and tools. A transparent map case attached to the top of your bar-bag is an ideal way of displaying maps and guidebook.

Your cycle should be fitted with mudguards and bell. It should be capable of carrying water bottles and pump. Except in June and July, lights are essential as Spain has a late sunrise and you are likely to start the day cycling in the dark. Many cyclists fit an odometer to measure distances. A basic toolkit should consist of puncture repair kit, spanners, Allen keys, adjustable spanner, screwdriver, spoke key and chain repair tool. The only essential spares are two spare tubes. On a long cycle ride, sometimes on dusty tracks, your chain will need regular lubrication and you should either carry a can of spray lube or make regular visits to cycle shops. A strong lock is advisable. Cycle helmets are compulsory in Spain, but the law is only loosely enforced.

SAFETY AND EMERGENCIES

Weather

The route passes through three distinct weather zones. The Pyrenees and Cantabrian mountains have an

Average temperatures (max/min °C)							
	Apr	May	Jun	Jul	Aug	Sep	Oct
Pamplona	16/5	20/9	25/12	28/14	28/15	25/12	19/9
León	15/3	19/7	24/10	27/12	27/12	23/10	17/7
Santiago	16/6	19/9	22/11	24/13	25/13	23/12	18/10

Average rainfall (mm/rainy days)							
	Apr	May	Jun	Jul	Aug	Sep	Oct
Pamplona	74/14	60/12	46/9	33/7	38/6	44/8	68/11
León	45/8	56/9	31/5	19/3	23/3	39/5	61/8
Santiago	146/14	135/13	72/8	43/6	57/6	107/8	226/14

Alpine climate with warm summers, cold winters and precipitation (rain in summer/snow in winter) at any time of year. Between these ranges, the high altitude meseta plateau has a continental climate (hot dry summers, cold wet winters). Spring and autumn mornings can be very cold before sunrise and gloves and woolly hat are essential. In Galicia, the climate is temperate oceanic with warm summers, mild winters and rain at any time of year.

Road safety

In Spain and France cycling is on the right side of the road. If you have never cycled before on the right you will quickly adapt, but roundabouts may prove challenging. You are most prone to mistakes when setting off each morning. Spain is a very

cycle-friendly country. Drivers will normally give you plenty of space when overtaking and often wait behind patiently until space to pass is available.

Although Spain is west of the Greenwich meridian, it uses Central European time making it one hour ahead of Britain. As far as natural light goes this is the 'wrong' time zone. As a result, on early spring and autumn mornings it remains dark until between 08.00 and 09.00. Most walkers start early, usually before 07.00, to avoid the heat of the day. As a result, they walk for several hours in the dark. Even with lights, this is not an option for cyclists where rough tracks and unlit walkers pose a major hazard. If you are cycling off-road on the camino route, do not start until it is bright enough to

For many kilometres the Camino follows sendas beside main roads (Stage 9)

see the track clearly without lights. In contrast, it remains light well into the evening and you should have no difficulty reaching your overnight stop before dark.

The camino route is mostly on tracks shared with a large number of walkers. Relations between walkers and cyclists can become strained, with some pedestrians believing that cyclists are wrongly using footpaths (you are not, the track is a bridleway for walkers and riders!). To ease this tension, cyclists should always be polite to walkers. Use your bell when approaching pedestrians from behind. If they do not hear you, shout '*Hola*' (hello) and travel slowly enough to take avoiding action if they step into your path. Many sections are on sendas, gravel tracks parallel to and beside main roads. Where these roads are quiet it is usually better for cyclists to use the road and leave the senda for pedestrians. On some of the hilly sections you will find rough and narrow rocky tracks. These can be slippery and dangerous to negotiate and are often filled with walkers picking their way slowly up or down the hill. As a result, they are not recommended for cyclists and this guide describes alternative routes that avoid such obstacles.

Most of the road route uses main roads. However, since the completion of the Spanish *autopista* (motorway) network, these roads are extremely quiet with very little traffic. Moreover, almost all Spanish main roads have

a metre-wide asphalt-surfaced hard shoulder which doubles as a cycle lane. Cycling is prohibited on motorways.

Many city and town centres have pedestrian only zones. These restrictions are often only loosely enforced and you may find locals cycling within them, indeed many zones have signs allowing cycling. One-way streets in Spain often have signs permitting contra-flow cycling but in some cases you will need to dismount and walk your cycle.

Health
No special injections or health precautions are needed for Spain, but it is advisable to make sure basic inoculations for tetanus, diphtheria and hepatitis are up to date. The greatest health risk comes from sunshine and heat, particularly crossing the meseta in July and August. Sun hat, sun screen, lip salve and plentiful supplies of water are essential. One particular irritation is from bed bugs in cheaper accommodation, but as bed bugs do not carry dangerous diseases their bites are an annoyance rather than a health risk. Spraying your bed sheet with permethrin before leaving home will give some protection, as will a specially treated fine-mesh undersheet, such as the Lifesystems bed bug sheet.

Emergencies
In the unlikely event of an accident, the standardised EU emergency

phone number is 112. The entire route has mobile phone coverage. Medical costs of EU citizens in possession of a valid EHIC card are covered under reciprocal health insurance agreements, although you may have to pay for an ambulance and claim the cost back through insurance. British citizens can obtain a GHIC card, which provides similar cover to an EHIC card.

Theft
In general, the route is safe and the risk of theft low. However, you should always lock your cycle and watch your belongings, especially in cities.

Insurance
Travel insurance policies usually cover you when cycle touring but they do not normally cover damage to, or theft of, your bicycle. If you have a household contents policy, this may cover cycle theft, but limits may be less than the actual cost of your cycle. Cycling UK (previously known as the Cyclists' Touring Club), www.ctc. org.uk, offers a policy tailored to the needs of cycle tourists.

ABOUT THIS GUIDE

Text and maps
There are 18 stages, each covered by separate maps drawn to a scale of 1:100,000. The camino route line is shown in red and the road route in blue. Short excursions to visit town centres or off-route points of interest are shown in orange. GPX files are

Walking and cycling peregrinos mostly share the same trails (Stage 6)

After Sarria the Camino becomes very busy with '100km walkers' who start in Sarria (Stages 16–18)

available on Cicerone's website at www.cicerone.co.uk/969/GPX.

All places shown on the maps appear in **bold** in the route description. Distances shown are cumulative kilometres within each stage, while altitudes shown in metres (m) are measured in the centre of the town or village. The abbreviation sp stands for 'signposted'. For each city/town/village passed an indication is given of facilities available (accommodation, albergue, youth hostel, refreshments, camping, tourist office, cycle shop, station) when the guide was written. This list is neither exhaustive nor does it guarantee that establishments are still in business. No attempt has been made to list all such facilities as this would require another book the same size as this one. For full accommodation listings, contact local tourist offices. Such listings are usually available online. There is a facilities summary table in Appendix A and details of tourist offices along the route are shown in Appendix B. Other useful contact details are given in Appendix E.

While route descriptions were accurate at the time of writing, things do change. Temporary diversions may be necessary to circumnavigate improvement works and permanent diversions to incorporate new sections of track. Where construction is in progress you may find signs showing recommended diversions, although these are likely to be in Spanish only.

Language

While Castilian Spanish is the national language of Spain, regional languages are widely spoken in parts of the country and you will

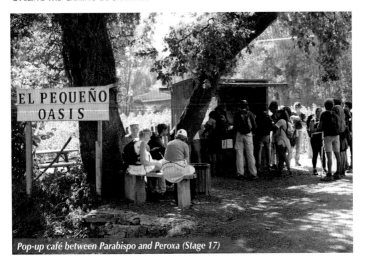

Pop-up café between Parabispo and Peroxa (Stage 17)

find Basque used in Navarre (Stages 1–4) and Galician in Galicia (Stages 15–18). In Navarre most towns have two names while in both these regions road signs are bi-lingual. In this guide, Castilian Spanish names are used throughout.

This guide is written for an English-speaking readership. Along the route of the Camino, most people working in the tourist industry speak at least a few words of English. However, any attempt to speak Spanish is usually warmly appreciated. The most common language used by peregrinos is English and you will find people of many nations communicating with each other in English. Appendix F contains a list of useful Castilian Spanish words.

THE ROUTE

The Camino follows narrow streets through Belorado (Stage 6)

STAGE 1
St Jean-Pied-de-Port to Roncesvalles

Start	St Jean-Pied-de-Port, office of Les Amis du Chemin de St Jacques (187m)
Finish	Roncesvalles abbey (948m)
Distance	28km; road route 27.5km
Ascent	1106m; road route 961m
Descent	345m; road route 200m

There is a choice of three routes to reach Puerto de Ibañeta. The most popular for walkers is the route Napoléon via col Lepoeder (1450m). This has a long, very steep road ascent (reaching a maximum gradient of 25 per cent), while the upper section, although less steep, is off-road on rough or grassy tracks. It is suitable only for very experienced mountain-bikers and then only in good weather. The lower less steep route via Valcarlos and the Ibañeta pass (1057m) has two variants, a walking route and a cycling route. The lower part of the walking route, which follows quiet roads as far as Valcarlos, is passable by all cyclists but the upper section on steep woodland paths is not recommended.

The camino route described below follows the walking route to Valcarlos then joins the road route over the pass, while the road route is on the well-surfaced pass road throughout. From Puerto de Ibañeta, both routes follow the main road descending slightly to Roncesvalles abbey.

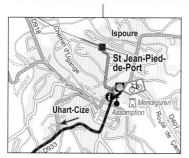

Getting to the start
From front of **St Jean-Pied-de-Port station** (157m), follow Rue de la Gare E, then fork R (Ave Renaud, sp Accueil des Pèlerins). Ave Renaud is one-way street with contra-flow cycling permitted. Bear L to reach T-junction. Turn L and immediately R (Pl du Trinquet) on ramp back beside main road. Turn L (Rue de

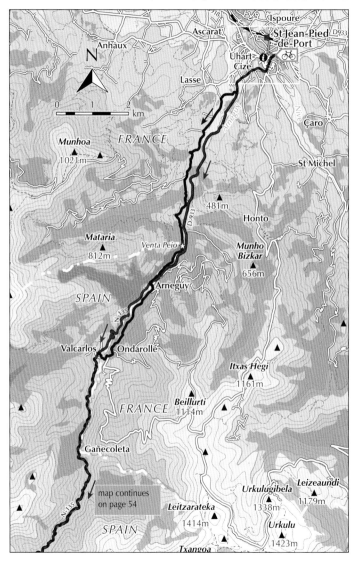

map continues on page 54

The streets in the old town are pedestrian only from 11.30 to 18.30.

From St Jean until the border the route is waymarked as 'Chemin de St Jacques' (French for Camino de Santiago).

France) through city walls into old town to reach T-junction. ◀ Turn L steeply uphill (cobbles) to soon reach office L of Les Amis du Chemin de St Jacques at 39 Rue de la Citadelle (**0.7km**, 187m).

Camino route

◀ From Les Amis du Chemin de St Jacques in **St Jean-Pied-de-Port** (accommodation, albergue, refreshments, camping, tourist office, cycle shop, station), follow

ST JEAN-PIED-DE-PORT

Rue de la Citadelle is lined with old houses

St Jean-Pied-de-Port (pop 1500) is a medieval walled town stretching along one main street that is the route of the Chemin de St Jacques. At the north end of town, the Chemin enters via the Porte St Jacques gate then passes many attractive old houses built in grey, pink or red sandstone and decorated with carvings showing the names and occupations of former residents. It leaves by crossing the river Nive on a so-called Roman bridge (actually medieval and restored in 1634) and passes through the Porte d'Espagne gate. Beside the bridge the Church of the Assumption and neighbouring houses with wooden balconies overhanging the river are much photographed. Above the town, the Mendiguren citadelle first built in the 12th century as a castle for the kings of Navarre was extended and strengthened in the 17th century by the French military engineer Vauban. There are walks along the ramparts but the fortress is occupied by a college and cannot be visited.

cobbled Rue de la Citadelle back downhill through old town past Church of the Assumption L and over river Nive, then ascend to reach Porte d'Espagne gate. Continue ahead (D301, sp St Michel) for 100 metres then turn R (D381, Ch de Mayorga) climbing out of town through **Uhart-Cize**.

Emerge onto main road (D933) and bear L. After 700 metres pass house 33 on L then fork R and cross river Arnéguy. ▶ Bear L at T-junction then go ahead over small crossroads. Fork sharply L at T-junction, winding through fields. Fork L downhill at next road junction. Pass between buildings of Mespia farm and after 100 metres fork R uphill through woods. At next junction fork L downhill and pass Carricaburia farm R. Continue through woods with short gravel section where road crosses unmarked Franco-Spanish border to reach carpark of **Venta Peio** (refreshments). ▶ Continue past shops, then bear R on red asphalt strip past service station (do not cross river) and follow winding track through woods to **Arnéguy** (**8.5km**, 256m) (accommodation, refreshments).

In centre of village drop down L on concrete ramp then dogleg L and R across main road and follow road bearing L over river Arnéguy, re-entering France. Turn R (D128, sp Ondarolle) uphill between wall of open *fronton* (Basque pelota court) R and church L. At end of village fork R, following lower road (D128) ascending gently above E side of river Luzaide. Pass through **Ondarolle** hamlet with Valcarlos on R bank, then fork R descending steeply. At bottom turn half-R on winding lane and

The road route continues ahead on the D933.

The former duty-free shopping complex of Venta Peio is in Spanish territory and attracts French customers with lower Spanish prices.

53

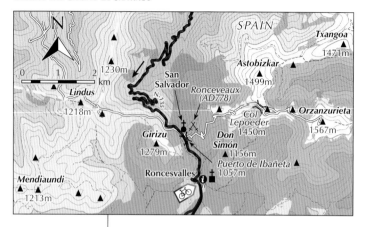

The road route rejoins here.

descend to cross river on narrow bridge (crossing border for final time) then ascend very steeply to reach main road in centre of **Valcarlos** (**11.5km**, 367m) (accommodation, albergue, refreshments). ◄

Turn L (N-135) and follow road ascending steadily through forest for 14km with views down into Luzaide valley L and up to Ibañeta pass high ahead. Cycle round seven hairpin bends to reach summit at **Puerto de Ibañeta** (**26.5km**, 1057m).

THE BATTLE OF RONCEVAUX

The Ibañeta pass (1057m), one of the lowest crossing points of the Pyrenees, is claimed to be the site of the Battle of Roncevaux (AD778). Here, as Charlemagne's Frankish army was returning to France after the siege of Zaragoza, its rear-guard was attacked by Basque guerrillas in retaliation for the destruction of the Basque capital Pamplona. All 3000 soldiers were killed, including the commander Roland. However, this delaying action enabled the rest of the army to escape unscathed to France. Subsequent legends have grown around these events, many of which describe it as a battle between Christian and Muslim forces (most of Spain including Zaragoza was under Moorish Muslim control) although the Basques were not Moors. It was claimed that the Franks were attacked by 400,000 Saracens and that Roland

The Roland stone on the Ibañeta pass commemorates the Battle of Roncevaux

blew a sacred horn (the Oliphant) to summon help but this arrived too late. Roland became a cult-hero figure and model for chivalric knights for many centuries. The *Song of Roland*, which describes the battle, was sung by medieval French pilgrims along the way. Written by an anonymous French 11th-century poet, it is regarded as the oldest known literary work in French. A memorial stone (erected 1967) commemorates Roland. The chapel of San Salvador and the summit cross are also 1960s' additions.

From summit, follow main road downhill round another hairpin to soon reach **Roncesvalles abbey (28km, 948m)** (accommodation, albergue, refreshments, tourist office).

Roncesvalles abbey has been providing pilgrim accommodation since the 13th century

Roncesvalles Augustinian abbey dates from the 13th century when the first buildings and the collegiate church were built on the orders of King Sancho VII of Navarre, who is buried in the chapter house. The museum and library hold religious and secular items together with items associated with Charlemagne and the legend of Roland. The monastery has a long history of providing accommodation and refreshments for pilgrims, reflected in numerous additions to the original core buildings. A pilgrim mass is held in the abbey church every evening.

Road route

From Les Amis du Chemin de St Jacques, follow cobbled Rue de la Citadelle back downhill through old town past Church of the Assumption L and over river Nive, then ascend to reach Porte d'Espagne gate. Continue ahead (D301, sp St Michel) for 100 metres then turn R (D381, Ch de Mayorga) climbing out of town through **Uhart-Cize**.

Emerge onto main road (D933) and bear L, at first descending slightly then ascending gently. Pass **Venta Peio** shopping complex (refreshments) on opposite bank of river R. Continue on main road through **Arnéguy** (**8km**, 256m) (accommodation, refreshments), where Franco-Spanish border is crossed, to reach

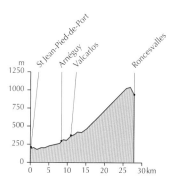

Valcarlos (**11km**, 367m) (accommodation, albergue, refreshments).

Continue on road (N-135) ascending steadily through forest for 14km with views down into Luzaide valley L and up to Ibañeta pass high ahead. Cycle round seven hairpin bends to reach summit at **Puerto de Ibañeta** (**26km**, 1057m). From summit, follow main road downhill round another hairpin to soon reach **Roncesvalles abbey** (**27.5km**, 948m) (accommodation, albergue, refreshments, tourist office).

Venta Peio duty-free shopping complex on the Spanish side of the French-Spanish border

STAGE 2
Roncesvalles to Pamplona

Start	Roncesvalles abbey (948m)
Finish	Pamplona town hall (457m)
Distance	42.5km; road route 46.5km
Ascent	491m; road route 316m
Descent	982m; road route 807m

After first undulating through the Pyrenean foothills, the stage descends steeply into the río Arga valley at Zubiri before following this valley gently downhill to Pamplona. The camino route mostly follows narrow tracks and field paths with some steep rocky sections. This route is passable by mountain bikes and hybrids but is tough going, particularly the descent to Zubiri. Unless you have off-road experience, you should follow the road route along the N-135, a quiet main road, for 38km, rejoining the Camino after Zabaldika.

Camino route
Opposite entrance to **Roncesvalles abbey** fork R on track downhill winding through forest more or less parallel with N-135 main road. Turn L at T-junction to reach main road then dogleg R and L across road to join track on opposite side, soon bearing R onto main road through **Burguete** (**3km**, 898m) (accommodation, refreshments). Towards end of village turn R steeply downhill beside Santander bank and go ahead over ford across río Urrobi. Pass barns of intensive farm R then bear L onto road and where this ends, bear L on rough track. Pass through gate and cross two smaller fords and continue ahead undulating through woods, crossing two more fords. ◄ Bear R onto road and follow this to beginning of built-up area and fork L to reach main road in **Espinal** (**6.5km**, 871m) (accommodation, albergue, refreshments, camping).

All these fords have narrow pedestrian bridges that you can use if the stream is high.

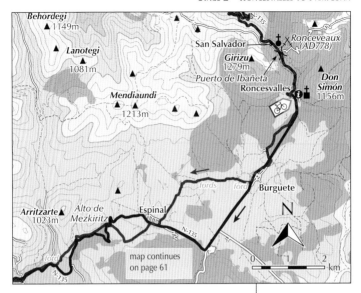

Turn R through village, then turn L beside house 32 onto road leading to track uphill through fields. Fork

Burguete ford and pedestrian bridge over the río Urrobi

Although shallow this ford is very slippery and can be avoided by joining main road and turning right and then right again (sp Sorogain) onto side road.

After Lintzoáin, the camino route and N-135 main road take different routes with the road descending to Erro.

R into woods, then follow track bearing R along ridge crest to reach main road at **Alto de Mezkíritz** (922m). Go ahead over road and fork immediately L into woods. Follow track bearing L and continue through woods with main road L. Briefly emerge beside road then bear R on track back into woods. Cycle downhill, then next time track reaches road, turn R just before road through shallow ford crossing río Erro to reach side road and turn R. ◄ After 50 metres fork L on concrete track parallel with main road L. At T-junction turn R and follow quiet road between houses, then cross main road into **Gerendiain** (**11.5km**, 782m) (accommodation, refreshments).

Follow road, turning sharply R in village, then after last house fork L on concrete track. Emerge beside main road, then fork L beside woods L. Follow track curving R, then dogleg L and R across main road and follow track into **Lintzoáin** (**13km**, 741m) (accommodation, refreshments). ◄

Turn R uphill in village under small wooden bridge then dogleg L and R over staggered crossing of tracks. Fork R, following rough rocky track winding through forest. Bear L at junction of tracks then continue ahead over next track crossing. Follow winding track contouring through forest. Continue for 3km past low summits of **El Fuerte** L and **Karrobide** R to reach communications masts and main road crossing at **Alto de Erro summit** (**17.5km**, 803m) (pop-up refreshments). Cross N-135 on track and soon fork R past ruins of **Ventas del Puerto** (medieval

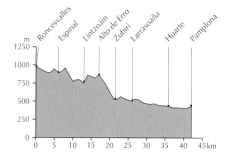

60

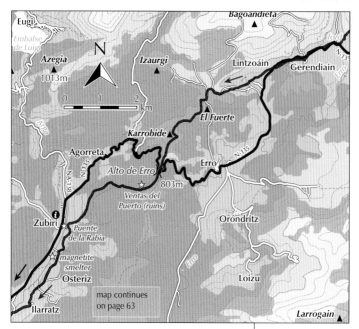

pilgrim hostel) R. Continue to wind through forest, eventually descending on steep rocky path to edge of **Zubiri** (**21km**, 532m) (accommodation, albergue, refreshments, tourist office). ▶

Fork L steeply uphill at beginning of village (do not cross river), then continue on track undulating through fields to reach T-junction. Turn R, then L at next T-junction on road passing large **magnetite smelter** across river R. ▶ Continue on road with magnetite quarries below R (walkers follow narrow track through tall grass R of road), then where road turns L away from quarries, continue ahead on broad track. Dogleg R and L across quarry road onto track steeply down L beside flight of steps. Continue on broad track and where this ends go ahead over small bridge with waterfall L and ascend to **Ilarratz** (**23.5km**, 549m).

To reach village centre, fork R on Puente de la Rabia bridge over río Arga.

Magnetite is a mineral that when burnt with charcoal produces magnesium oxide, a refractory material used to line furnaces, incinerators and kilns.

The magnetite smelter at Zubiri produces refractory material for lining furnaces

To reach village centre, turn R over Puente de los Bandidos bridge.

Turn R at mini-roundabout on road downhill out of hamlet then turn L uphill on apex of second bend (sp Ezkirotz). Continue past **Ezkirotz** (albergue) and follow shady track winding through fields. Go ahead over crossroads and continue past **Larrasoaña** R (**26.5km**, 503m) (accommodation, albergue, refreshments) on opposite side of Arga. ◄

Turn L at T-junction away from bridge and follow rough track ascending to **Akerreta** (accommodation). Fork R in village onto shady track descending between fields. Dogleg L and R over staggered crossroads into forest, then descend to reach Arga. Follow riverside track to reach T-junction and turn R across bridge into **Zuriain** (**30km**, 476m) (albergue, refreshments).

Turn L onto main road (N-135, cycle lane R) and follow this for 600 metres. Turn L (sp Ilúrdotz) then cross river and fork R. Where road ends by old mine L, bear L on track first through forest then scrubland to reach **Irotz** (**32km**, 476m) (refreshments).

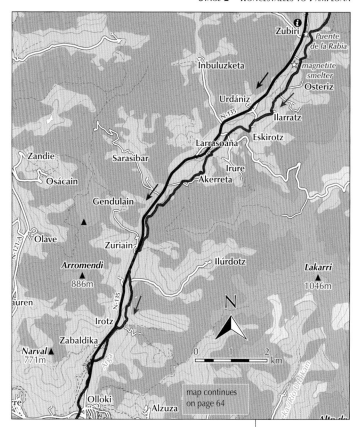

Bear R on road, then fork R beside church and follow road bearing R over river. Immediately after bridge
turn L on road passing bathing beach L. Continue parallel with river then pass under road bridge and turn L at
T-junction. Cross river and turn immediately R on concrete track parallel with river R. Briefly emerge beside
main road. ▸ Bear R to continue beside river then pass
under road bridge and fork R to continue on concrete
track. Pass new industrial estate L then turn R on wooden

The road route
joins here.

63

bridge over river. Pass rocky waterfall L and bear R through barriers (Ibaialde) on narrow cobbled road winding between houses. At end bear R (Calle Zubiarte) and continue through **Huarte** (**36.5km**, 445m) (accommodation, albergue, refreshments).

At end of town, fork L downhill (sp Villava) and cross Arga on stone bridge. ◄ At pedestrian crossing, turn R beside allotments, then continue over another river bridge and turn L beside main road. After 350 metres, turn sharply L through red and white posts then turn immediately R and pass under road bridge. Continue beside Arga, then follow track bearing R on bridge over río Ulzama and continue beside river L. Pass under road bridge, continuing ahead. Pass sports arena and swimming pools R and pass under another road bridge, continuing beside river. Emerge onto road and bear L (Carretera de Burlada). Follow this forking R, then bear L (Camino de la Chantrea). At end turn R (cycle track L) then L on Puente de la Magdalena stone arch bridge over Arga.

At end of bridge bear R and go ahead across two roads at light-controlled crossings. Turn R and follow concrete track forking L in parkland beside ramparts of Caballo Blanco bastion L. Continue onto cobbled road

This left fork is easy to miss: it is opposite a black cube-like building covered with netting.

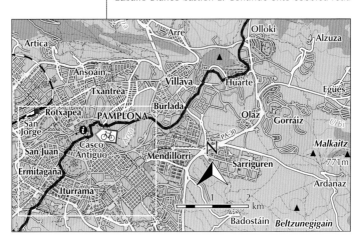

ascending through Portal de Francia gateway then follow road bearing L through archway into **Casco Antiguo** (old city). Continue ahead (Calle del Carmen) past Fuente de Navarreria fountain L into Calle Navarreria. Turn half-R at five-way junction (Calle de los Mercaderes) to reach Plaza Consistorial in front of town hall in **Pamplona** (**42.5km**, 457m) (accommodation, albergue, refreshments, tourist office, cycle shop, station).

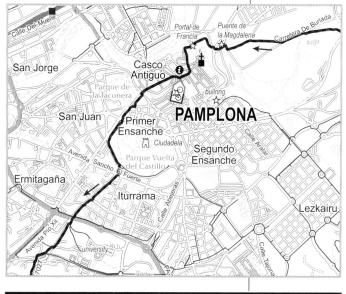

PAMPLONA

Pamplona (pop 196,000), the capital of Navarre, is known worldwide for El Encierro, the annual running of the bulls. Originally established by the Vascones (Basques) as Iruña, it became a Roman city in 75BC under General Pompey, who gave his name to the city as Pompaelo, which became Pamplona. After the Romans left, control alternated between Visigoths, Basques, Franks and Moors before the city became part of Spain in 1512. The oldest religious buildings including the cathedral are Gothic, reflecting Frankish influence,

A monument in Pamplona celebrating 'El Encierro'

while many other religious buildings are in Spanish Baroque style.

The city was strongly fortified with the large Ciudadela citadel on the southwest flank and fortified bastions on the other three sides. The city remained within these walls until the early 20th century, by which time advances in artillery had made them redundant. Part of the walls were demolished in 1915 and development of residential areas around the city began. Industry was late coming to Pamplona, with the main employer Volkswagen arriving in the 1970s, although nowadays the city is one of the wealthiest in Spain.

Pamplona has the second largest bullring in Spain seating nearly 20,000 spectators. The San Fermin Festival is held annually 6–14 July. Every morning during the festival six bulls are run through the streets to the bullring for the afternoon bullfight. Daredevil participants run ahead of the bulls, usually dressed in white shirts and red scarves. Since Ernest Hemingway described it in *The Sun also Rises*, this event has become a popular tourist attraction. Unfortunately, it often leads to serious injuries and there have been 15 deaths in the last 100 years.

Road route

From Roncesvalles abbey, follow N-135 S gently downhill through **Burguete** (**2.5km**, 898m) (accommodation, refreshments) to **Espinal** (**6.5km**, 871m) (accommodation, albergue, refreshments, camping). After short ascent to **Alto de Mezkíritz** (922m), road continues downhill past **Gerendiain** (**12.5km**, 780m) (accommodation, refreshments) to **Erro** (**17.5km**, 659m) then rises via series of hairpin bends to col at **Alto de Erro** (**20.5km**, 801m) (pop-up refreshments). Descend steadily through forest round more hairpins past **Agorreta** into Arga valley at **Zubiri** (**26.5km**, 530m) (accommodation, albergue, refreshments, tourist office) then continue gently

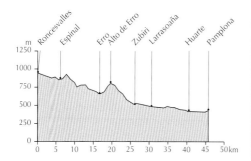

downhill along valley passing **magnetite smelter** L. Fork R to pass through **Urdániz** R (**29km**, 510m) (albergue) returning to main road after village and then fork L to pass through **Larrasoaña** L (**31km**, 500m) (accommodation, albergue, refreshments) again returning to main road. Continue through **Zuriain** (**34.5km**, 476m) (albergue, refreshments).

Pass **Zabaldika** (**37km**, 478m) (albergue) then after 1km fork R on concrete cycle track beside river R, joining camino route. ▶ Continue beside river then pass under road bridge and fork R to continue on concrete track. Pass new industrial estate L then turn R on wooden bridge over river. Pass rocky waterfall L and bear R through barriers (Ibaialde) on narrow cobbled road winding between houses. Bear R (Calle Zubiarte) and continue through **Huarte** (**40.5km**, 445m) (accommodation, albergue, refreshments).

At end of town, fork L downhill (sp Villava) and cross Arga on stone bridge. ▶ At pedestrian crossing, turn R beside allotments, then continue over another river bridge and turn L beside main road. After 350 metres, turn sharply L through red and white posts then turn immediately R and pass under road bridge. Continue beside Arga, then follow track bearing R on bridge over río Ulzama and continue beside river L. Pass under road bridge, continuing ahead. Pass sports arena and swimming pools R and pass under another road bridge,

This right fork is easy to miss: it is just before a wayside cross.

The left fork is easy to miss: it is opposite a black cube-like building covered with netting.

The elegant Puente de Magdalena bridge over the río Arga is below the city walls of Pamplona

continuing beside river. Emerge onto road and bear L (Carretera de Burlada). Follow this forking R, then bear L (Camino de la Chantrea). At end turn R (cycle track L) then L on Puente de la Magdalena stone arch bridge over Arga.

At end of bridge bear R and go ahead across two roads at light-controlled crossings. Turn R and follow concrete track forking L in parkland beside ramparts of Caballo Blanco bastion L. Continue onto cobbled road ascending through Portal de Francia gateway then follow road bearing L through archway into **Casco Antiguo** (old city). Continue ahead (Calle del Carmen) past Fuente de Navarreria fountain L into Calle Navarreria. Turn half-R at five-way junction (Calle de los Mercaderes) to reach Plaza Consistorial in front of town hall in **Pamplona** (**46.5km**, 457m) (accommodation, albergue, refreshments, tourist office, cycle shop, station).

STAGE 3
Pamplona to Estella

Start	Pamplona town hall (457m)
Finish	Estella, palace of the Kings of Navarre (423m)
Distance	45km; road route 48.5km
Ascent	814m; road route 704m
Descent	848m; road route 738m

After leaving Pamplona the Camino, mostly on gravel field paths, ascends steeply to reach a windswept pass at Alto del Perdón then descends into the Arga valley. The río Arga is crossed at Puente la Reina, after which the route climbs onto a plateau and undulates through arable fields before descending to the medieval pilgrim town of Estella. The road route mostly follows the NA-1110 (former N-111). Since the A-12 motorway opened this has become a very quiet main road with almost no traffic.

Camino route

From Plaza Consistorial in front of town hall in **Pamplona**, follow Calle San Saturnino W, passing San Saturnino church L, and continue into Calle Mayor. At end pass San Lorenzo church L then go ahead over crossroads and join cycle track L of road just inside Taconera park, parallel with Calle del Bosquecillo. Go ahead over dual carriageway (Calle Navas de Tolosa) and turn R on cycle track L of road parallel with Ave Pio XII R. Continue over another dual carriageway with Ciudadela citadel in park L following cycle track beside road then bearing L beside Calle de la Vuelta del Castillo. Turn R across road at third crossing into Calle Fuente del Hierro.

Go ahead over crossroads and join cycle track L. Continue over two roundabouts and under road bridge. Pass mini-roundabout and fork R to follow cycle track beside Carretera de la Universidad. Turn R across road

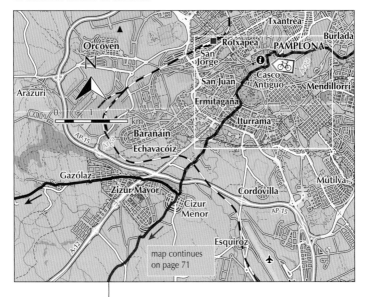

at crossing and continue R of road, passing roundabout L. Pass wayside cross R then turn L across road and continue over río Sadar. Follow cycle track ahead (sp Cizur Menor), R of road. Cross railway bridge and go ahead at small roundabout. Continue over motorway uphill to reach **Cizur Menor** (**5km**, 466m) (albergue, refreshments).

To follow road route, turn R at second roundabout.

Bear R at first mini-roundabout (Calle Irun Bidea) and go ahead at second (Calle Esparza Bidea). ◀ Just

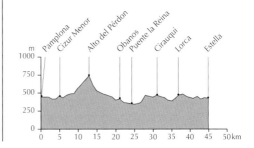

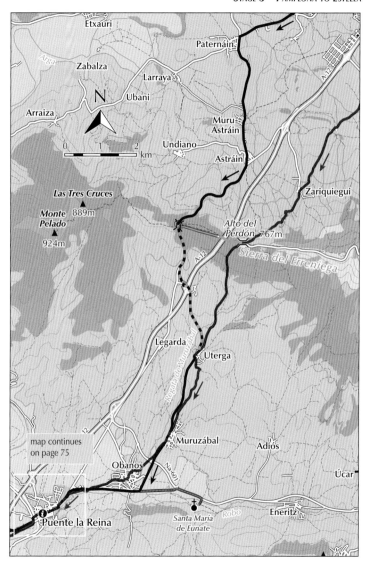

map continues
on page 75

*San Andrés church
in Zariquiegui*

after next road junction R, fork R on tree-lined cycle track. Go ahead at crossroads (Calle Santiago Bidea) to reach T-junction, then continue ahead on cycle track into open country. Emerge on road and continue ahead past **Zizur Mayor** R. At end of village, join track L of road and follow this bearing L between fields. Go ahead over two crossroads then fork R at track junction and ascend steadily through fields passing ruins of Guenduláin castle across fields R to reach **Zariquiegui** (**11km**, 627m) (albergue, refreshments). Go ahead over crossroads and continue through village into open fields. Bear L at junction of tracks and ascend steeply to reach col at **Alto del Perdón** (**13km**, 767m).

At **Alto del Perdón**, the route crosses the high ridge of the Sierra del Erreniega with extensive views in all directions. This location is notoriously exposed, with 40 turbines along the ridge taking advantage of the wind. A spectacular monument erected in 1996 titled '*Donde se cruza el camino del viento con el de las estrellas*' (Where the path of the wind crosses that of the stars) shows a line of rusty (originally

black) cast-iron medieval pilgrims traversing the ridge.

Pilgrim statues at Alto del Perdón

Descend from ridge on a steep and rocky track, which can be slippery in wet weather and is often occupied by walkers slowly making their way down. ▶

An alternative road route is available (adding 2.5km).

Alto del Perdón to Uterega avoiding rocky descent
Turn R along ridgetop, descending to cross bridge over NA-1110 road then turn R steeply downhill on main road. Bear R into turning lane then turn L across main road (unsigned). After 500 metres, turn R down concrete ramp to reach roundabout. Turn L (third exit, sp Uterga) then pass under motorway and go ahead (second exit, sp Uterga) at next roundabout. Turn R at T-junction into **Uterga**.

Cross ridgetop road and descend very steeply on rough track. After 650 metres, cycle route bears R (signposted) to avoid most difficult section, rejoining walkers route after 100 metres. At bottom of descent cross bridge over small stream and continue through fields to **Uterga** (**17km**, 492m) (albergue, refreshments).

Go ahead (Calle Mayor) through village then fork L (Calle Mediodía) and bear R. Where road ends, continue downhill on track between fields. After 225 metres, cross small stream and turn R. Follow track between fields to emerge on road and follow this through **Muruzábal** L (**19.5km**, 442m) (albergue, refreshments). Just before end of village, fork R onto track and follow this under road bridge and uphill to reach beginning of Obanos. Fork R (Calle Roncesvalles), then turn L opposite house 15 (Calle San Juan). Turn immediately R (Calle Julian Gayarre) and L (Camino San Lorenzo) to reach Plaza de los Fueros in centre of **Obanos** (**21km**, 414m) (accommodation, albergue, refreshments).

Pass church R, then go ahead through arch and bear R between modern fronton court L and church R. Go ahead over staggered crossroads and bear L (Calle San Salvador). Continue into Calle Camino de Santiago out of village. Where road ends go ahead on track descending to cross main road and continue on track to reach beginning of Puente la Reina. Bear L on road and turn L through Jakue hotel carpark to join main road (NA-1110). After 300 metres, turn L (Plaza Padre Guillermo Zicke) and R under archway beside Church of the Crucifixion (Calle del Crucifijo) into centre of **Puente la Reina** (**24km**, 351m) (accommodation, albergue, refreshments, camping, tourist office).

Puente la Reina (pop 3000) is named after the Romanesque Queen's bridge over the río Arga, one

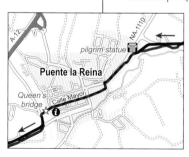

of the most attractive bridges on the Camino. The six-arched bridge was built to the order of Queen Muniadona (995–1066), wife of King Sancho III, specifically to aid pilgrims crossing the river. The town is the junction with another medieval pilgrim route, the Camino Aragonese, which brought pilgrims from Catalonia, southern France and Italy. A modern statue

of an ancient pilgrim stands beside this junction, east of town.

Go ahead through town on cobbled Calle Mayor and continue over Arga on Puente la Reina bridge. Turn L beside river then go ahead over crossroads and bear R passing Comendadoras convent L. At end of town, where road becomes one-way, fork L on gravel

Puente la Reina bridge was built to aid medieval pilgrims

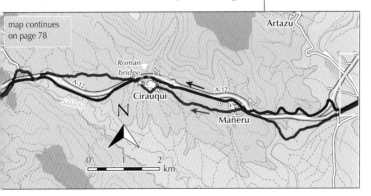

map continues on page 78

75

The Camino approaching the hilltop town of Cirauqui

track then continue under road bridge into open country. Fork R to pass sewerage works L then cross small stream and ascend steeply winding through woodland. Emerge beside main road and follow track to roundabout. Bear L over first exit then follow second exit (Calle Mikelaldea) downhill into **Mañeru** (**28.5km**, 454m) (albergue, refreshments).

The waymarked walkers' route, which is not suitable for cyclists, follows a zigzag route through narrow alleyways over the top of the hill then descends a flight of steps to cross the Roman bridge.

Fork R over stream and follow Calle de la Esperanza to Plaza de los Fueros. Bear L and turn R to follow Calle Forzosa out of village. Where road ends beside cemetery, continue ahead on track ascending through fields and vineyards to hilltop village of **Cirauqui** (**31km**, 471m) (albergue, refreshments). ◀

Alternative route avoiding steps to Roman bridge
At beginning of village fork R in front of barn with corrugated iron double doors. Turn R (Calle Bidegorria). Go ahead (Calle Iguste) over crossroads and continue over another crossroads to reach roundabout. Turn L (third exit, NA-1110) parallel with motorway R, then 100 metres before road overbridge, turn L on gravel track.

At beginning of village, fork L in front of barn with corrugated iron double doors. Turn second R (Calle Cruces) then L (Calle Sarriozar). Continue into Calle Larreria and at end of town fork L downhill. Descend steps and cross Roman bridge. Ascend to reach road and turn sharply L on gravel track.

Follow track curving R to pass over motorway. Turn L on vehicular track winding through vineyards. ▶ Go ahead over crossing of tracks then fork L off vehicular track at next junction. After 400 metres, turn R across another vehicular track, winding downhill. Turn L at T-junction and pass under motorway. Bear R beside NA-1110 main road then turn R (sp Alloz) on quiet road back under motorway using track L. Pass under modern Alloz irrigation canal aqueduct and bear L then turn L on medieval bridge, crossing río Salado. Continue under motorway for third time then fork L on track parallel with but below main road. Follow this, ascending to **Lorca** (**36.5km**, 463m) (albergue, refreshments).

Cycle through village on Calle Mayor, then bear L beside N-111 on track L. After 1km follow track bearing L away from road then fork R and after 150 metres turn R, continuing between fields. Join vehicular track then after 400 metres turn L beside small stream. Follow track under motorway into **Villatuerta** (**41km**, 423m) (albergue, refreshments).

Turn L (Calle Erregueta) then R opposite sports centre, passing around Plaza Mayor, and L (Calle San Ginés). At end bear R on bridge over río Iranzu and turn L (Rúa Nueva). Follow this bearing R uphill past church L and continue on Camino de Estella to T-junction. Go ahead on track through fields then bear L through woods parallel with NA-1110 R passing **ermita San Miguel chapel** L. Pass under NA-132 and follow winding track descending to cross río Ega. Continue past large bodega L to join road (Calle Curtidores). Pass Santo Sepulcro church L and pass under road bridge. Follow Calle de la Rúa to reach Palace of the Kings of Navarre facing Plaza de San Martin in **Estella** (**45km**, 423m) (accommodation, albergue, youth hostel, refreshments, camping, tourist office, cycle shop).

The waymarked walkers' route follows a narrow track just to the right and slightly above the main track.

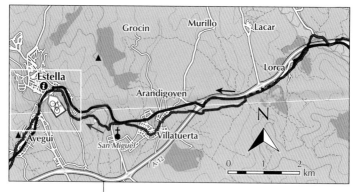

Founded in 1090, **Estella** (pop 14,000) became prosperous as an important town on the medieval Camino with a bridge over the río Ega and many ancient churches, monasteries and secular buildings. A number of these are in Romanesque style from the 11th and 12th centuries, built under the patronage and influence of French pilgrims. Most notable are the churches of Santo Sepulcro (now a pilgrimage museum), San Miguel Arcángel and San Pedro de la Rúa. The Palace of the Kings of Navarre is the only extant Romanesque palace in Spain.

Road route

Follow camino route out of **Pamplona** as far as second roundabout in **Cizur Menor** (**5km**, 466m) (albergue, refreshments). Turn R (first exit, NA-6053) and follow road to **Zizur Mayor** (accommodation, refreshments). Go ahead R (NA-8108) over motorway bridge and continue ahead over three roundabouts using cycle track L. Fork R to pass through **Gazólaz** (**8.5km**, 458m), then rejoin main road after village. At crossroads just before **Paternáin** (**10.5km**, 436m) (refreshments), turn L (sp

Astráin, NA-7010) and follow road ascending stead-ily through **Muru-Astráin** and **Astráin** (refreshments) (**14km**, 525m).

At end of village bear R (NA-1110) and climb steeply onto wooded ridge with line of wind turbines along crest to reach summit (**17km**, 685m). Descend steeply then turn first L onto unsigned side road. After 500 metres, turn R down concrete ramp to reach roundabout. Turn L (third exit, sp Uterga) then pass under motorway and go ahead (NA-6016, second exit, sp Uterga) at next round-about. Turn R (Calle Mayor) through **Uterga** (**21km**, 492m) (albergue, refreshments).

The unusual 12th-century octagonal church at Eunate lies 2km off-route

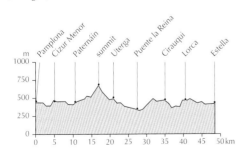

To visit octagonal
Santa María church
at Eunate turn L at
T-junction and follow
NA-6064 towards
Campanas for 2km.

Go ahead through village and continue downhill through **Muruzábal** (**23.5km**, 442m) (albergue, refreshments). Pass under road bridge and continue past **Obanos** on hillside R to reach T-junction. ◀ Turn R (NA-6064, sp Puente la Reina) and continue to beginning of Puente la Reina. Fork L (sp Excepto hoteles) and after 250 metres turn I through Jakue hotel carpark to join main road (NA-1110). After 300 metres, turn L (Plaza Padre Guillermo Zicke) and R (Calle del Crucifijo) under archway beside Church of the Crucifixion into centre of **Puente la Reina** (**27.5km**, 351m) (accommodation, albergue, refreshments, camping, tourist office).

Go ahead through town on cobbled Calle Mayor and continue over Arga on Puente la Reina bridge. Turn L beside river then turn R onto NA-1110 and continue to roundabout. Take second exit (NA-1110, sp Estella) ascending to pass under motorway bridge then bear L beside motorway and continue ascending through forest. Cross back over motorway, then go ahead at roundabout (first exit) bypassing **Mañeru** (**32.5km**, 473m) (albergue, refreshments). Continue parallel with motorway and go ahead over roundabout (third exit) past **Cirauqui** (**35km**, 470m) (albergue, refreshments). Go ahead (second exit) at next roundabout, continuing beside motorway. Pass motorway junction and turn-off for Embalse de Alloz dam (both R), then fork L (NA-8408) uphill into **Lorca** (**40.5km**, 463m) (albergue, refreshments).

Cycle through village and rejoin NA-1110. Go ahead over first roundabout and ahead again at second, passing under motorway. Turn L at T-junction and continue past **Villatuerta** (**45km**, 445m) (albergue, refreshments) to reach beginning of Estella. Where road bears L to cross río Ega, continue ahead (Calle Espoz y Mina) then turn first L over Puente de la Cárcel medieval bridge. At end of bridge, turn R (Calle de la Rúa, cobbled) to reach Palace of the Kings of Navarre facing Plaza de San Martin in **Estella** (**48.5km**, 423m) (accommodation, albergue, youth hostel, refreshments, camping, tourist office, cycle shop).

STAGE 4
Estella to Logroño

Start	Estella, palace of the Kings of Navarre (423m)
Finish	Logroño, Santiago church (382m)
Distance	48.5km; road route 46km
Ascent	863m; road route 660m
Descent	904m; road route 701m

A steady ascent from Estella to the hillside village of Villamayor de Monjardin is followed by a long descent to Los Arcos and a gently undulating ride to Torres del Río. A steep climb over a scrubby ridge precedes a final descent through Viana to Logroño, capital of the Rioja wine-producing region. There is little or no shade as the route uses mostly field tracks through arable land with some vineyards, particularly towards the end. The road route uses the NA-1110 throughout.

Camino route
From Palace of the Kings of Navarre in **Estella**, follow Calle San Nicolás SW. Pass through Portal del Castillo gateway and continue on Camino de Logroño to

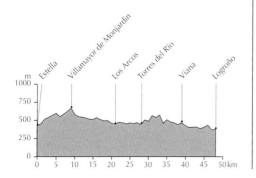

The fuente de vino *(wine fountain) at Bodegas Irache serves up 100 litres of free red wine to peregrinos every day*

The road route continues ahead on the NA-1110.

roundabout. Go ahead (Calle de Carlos VII), using service road R, to second roundabout. Bear R ahead on concrete track between first and second exits. ◄ Follow this through housing development and over two crossroads. Emerge on road and follow this (Calle Camino de Estella) uphill into **Ayegui** (**1.5km**, 502m) (albergue, refreshments).

Cycle through village on Calle Camino Santiago, then fork L beside house 30 into Calle Mayor. Turn L downhill by house 25 (Calle San Pelayo) and bear R (Calle Zuloandia). At bottom of hill, turn R on main road (NA-1110) then fork immediately L onto gravel track

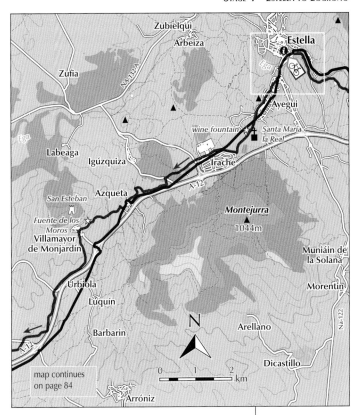

map continues
on page 84

ascending to pass between Bodegas Irache winery R and
Santa María la Real monastery L. ▶ Continue ascending to junction of tracks and turn R (Ave Prado). Cross
main road at staggered junction and continue past hotel L
into **Irache** (**4km**, 564m) (accommodation, refreshments,
camping).

Cycle through village and where road ends continue
on gravel track under road bridge and through fields
and forest. Cross minor road and follow track winding
through forest, then descend into small valley. Bear R

Bodegas Irache has
a museum of wine
and a wine fountain
where you can
sample their output
– or maybe not if you
have a long day in the
saddle ahead of you!

83

at junction of tracks then turn L at T-junction and follow track to **Azqueta** (**7km**, 581m) (albergue, refreshments).

Turn R at T-junction and follow road (Calle Carrera) bearing L through village. Just before reaching main road, fork R on concrete track. Turn sharply L by farm building and follow gravel track winding uphill through fields. Pass **Fuente de los Moros** R then bear R on concrete track. Go ahead at crossroads, bearing R (Calle Santa Maria) into **Villamayor de Monjardín** (**9km**, 676m) (accommodation, albergue, refreshments).

Road becomes cobbles, passing church L. Turn first L downhill and at end of village fork R, then R again on gravel track with occasional steps continuing downhill beside vineyard. Bear R onto vehicular track and follow this winding through fields. Cross two asphalt roads then fork R at junction of tracks (pop-up refreshments). Bear

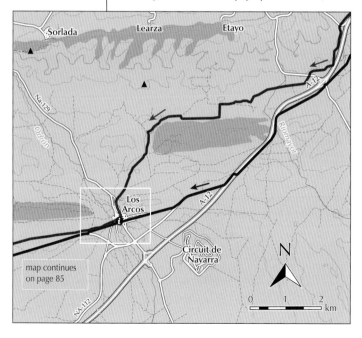

map continues on page 85

R at next junction, continuing with scrub covered hillside R. Where scrub ends, turn L downhill, and follow track as it curves R. Turn L at T-junction and bear L at junction of tracks. Pass over small bridge then turn L again at next T-junction and R at crossing of tracks. Emerge on road and fork L (Calle Mayor) beside house 116 into **Los Arcos** (**21km**, 445m) (accommodation, albergue, refreshments, tourist office).

Where arcaded building blocks street, turn R (Plaza de la Fruta) and continue through Plaza Santa María with church L. Go ahead under arch, then cross main road and bridge over river. Where road ends, continue straight ahead on track through fields. After 3.5km, turn R just past small vineyard. ▸ Cross next track and continue ahead for another 1.75km to reach quiet road. Turn L and follow road uphill to **Sansol** (**27.5km**, 493m) (accommodation, albergue, refreshments).

This right turn is easy to miss.

Pass through village on Carretera Desojo and turn R on NA-1110 (cycle track L). Where road curves R, turn L and immediately R on track steeply downhill. Pass under

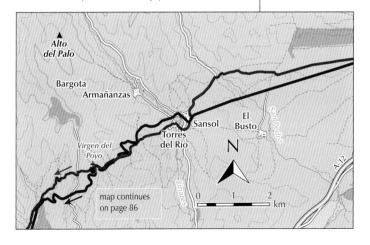

map continues on page 86

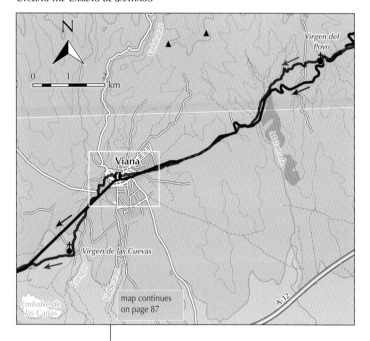

road bridge then cross río Linares to reach **Torres del Río** (**28.5km**, 464m) (albergue, refreshments).

Go ahead very steeply uphill into village (Calle Jesús Ordóñez), then turn L in front of church (Calle Mayor). Follow this curving R and L (still Calle Mayor) and go ahead out of village. Where road ends beside cemetery, continue ahead on gravel track through fields. Go ahead over staggered crossing of tracks and continue steeply uphill to reach NA-1110 road. Follow track L of road, crossing to R after 450 metres, then continue on R passing behind **ermita de la Virgen del Poyo chapel**.

Join road and follow this round sharp bend L, then turn R on track winding steeply up hillside. Emerge on road and turn L, then after 75 metres turn sharply R on gravel track. Follow this winding steeply downhill through scrubland. Cross road and ascend steeply through vineyards to reach road again. Bear L and follow road for 200 metres, then fork L on track parallel with road. Rejoin road, this time for 1km passing vineyards, then bear L again on parallel gravel track. Turn L at T-junction and continue to reach road at beginning of Viana. Turn L and after 75 metres fork R on asphalt path then continue on road (Calle el Cristo) between houses. At

end turn L and immediately sharply R uphill, then bear L through line of old town walls. Go ahead over crossroads and through archway (Calle Algarrada). Turn first L to reach Plaza del Coso and immediately R (Rúa de Santa María) through centre of **Viana** (**39km**, 471m) (accommodation, albergue, refreshments, tourist office).

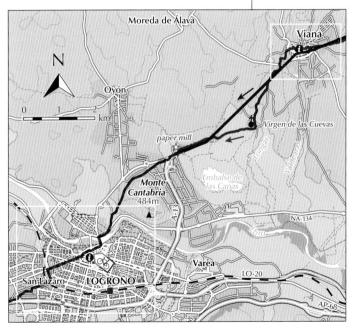

VIANA

Viana (pop 4000) was established in 1219 by Sancho VII as a fortified border town between his Kingdom of Navarre and neighbouring Castile. Over the centuries, frequent wars between these kingdoms led to regular changes of ownership. During one of these wars, King Juan of Navarre hired Cesare Borgia (1475–1507) who had fled from Italy after the death of his father Pope Alexander VI, to command his army. Unfortunately, during a siege of Viana, Cesare was captured and killed. He was buried in a mausoleum inside Santa María church. Some years later, the local bishop decided that it was inappropriate to venerate a man of dubious character and the remains were moved to a grave beneath the street in front of the church so that 'the feet of men and beasts would trample on his sins'. He was exhumed again in 1945 and is now buried beneath a marble slab by the church's west door.

There are many historic buildings in the old town, both religious and secular, including the town hall and noble houses emblazoned with carved stone shields. The Plaza del Coso, overlooked by the Balcón de Toros, was formerly an urban bullring.

At end, bear R (Plaza San Pedro) then turn L (Calle San Felices) through old city gate. Where this ends, go ahead over pedestrian crossing and turn immediately L downhill (Calle la Rueda). Turn second R (Calle Fuente Vieja) then cross main road continuing downhill and fork L (Paraje el Arenal) on road that soon becomes gravel track. Follow this winding out of town past allotments and across asphalt road. Continue ahead then bear L parallel with main road and drop down to pass under road and continue on other side. After 100 metres bear L on quiet road through vineyards, soon forking R between rows of vines. Cross stream and pass **ermita de la Virgin de las Cuevas chapel** R.

This footbridge has steps with a steep ramp for pushing cycles. To avoid it, turn L before wood and follow rough track beside wood R to reach and cross road.

Go ahead over crossing of tracks and after 50 metres bear R. Follow track through fields and into small wood, then cross NA-1110 road by footbridge. ◄ Follow track L beside NA-1110, passing **Saicapack paper mill** R. ◄ Cycle under four road bridges and continue through vineyards with Monte Cantabria rising L. Cross main road and turn R on promenade beside río Ebro. Immediately

The road route rejoins here.

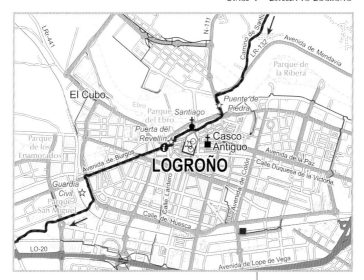

before bridge, turn back R up ramp to road and L across Puente de Piedra bridge. Turn half-R at roundabout (Calle Ruavieja, cobbles, second exit), then go ahead over crossroads to reach Santiago church in old part of **Logroño** (**48.5km**, 382m) (accommodation, albergue, refreshments, camping, tourist office, cycle shop, station).

LOGROÑO

Logroño (pop 150,000), which has a medieval centre surrounded by one of the fastest growing cities in northern Spain, started as a Roman settlement beside a crossing point of the Ebro. Later in medieval times this location became important again as the place where pilgrims on the Camino crossed the river. The oldest part of the town (Calle Ruavieja and Calle de Barriocepo) developed beside the route pilgrims took along the south bank of the river with pilgrim hospital and hostels. When the pilgrimage declined these streets became derelict as commercial activity moved away from the river. However, 20th-century revival of the Camino has led to a rebirth of this area with many old buildings restored.

Logroño cathedral

The restored Church of Santiago on Calle de Barriocepo has an enormous statue of St James the Moor-slayer above its main portal. When the city walls were demolished one gateway was retained, Puerta del Revellín where the Camino left the old city. The most attractive street is arcaded Calle Portales, where you will find the cathedral and market square, while Calle San Juan and Calle del Laurel with a large number of bars, tapas bars and restaurants are the places to go in the evening. The old city becomes particularly raucous during Logroño's two annual festivals: San Bernabé and San Mateo. The one-day (11 June) feast of San Bernabé celebrates the victory of the Logroñés over an invading French army after a siege in 1521. Participants dress in period clothes and organise parades and re-enactments. Fried trout, bread and wine are consumed as these are said to be the only foods that were available available during the siege. The much larger feast of San Mateo lasts for one week in mid to late September. Events, which celebrate the successful harvest, include wine treading and tastings, bullfights, fireworks and food battles using 'weapons' such as tomatoes, eggs, flour and mustard. Much local Rioja wine is consumed together with Zurracapote, a local stronger version of Sangría made from red wine and fermenting fruit such as oranges, lemons and peaches.

Beware, accommodation is hard to find during festivals! If you cycle through the old town during this period, watch out for broken glass on the streets!

Road route
Leave **Estella** on NA-1110 (sp Ayegui) ascending steeply through **Ayegui** (albergue, refreshments) and **Irache** (**3.5km**, 570m) (accommodation, refreshments,

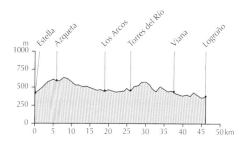

camping). Go ahead over roundabout (sp Los Arcos) and fork R to pass through **Azqueta** (**6.5km**, 577m) (albergue, refreshments). ▶ Rejoin NA-1110 after village and continue to summit (620m), with Villamayor de Monjardín visible across vineyards R. Follow NA-1110 L and R through two roundabouts crossing A-12 motorway and continue downhill on other side. Pass **Urbiola** (**9.5km**, 597m) (refreshments) and after 6km go under motorway. Fork R (NA-8401, sp Los Arcos) and cycle through **Los Arcos** (**19km**, 448m) (accommodation, albergue, refreshments, tourist office) and over río Odrón.

The main road passes through a tunnel under the village.

Vineyards surround Villamayor de Montjardin with San Esteban castle on the hilltop above

After village, rejoin NA-1110 and continue ahead, passing between **Sansol** R (**25km**, 487m) (accommodation, albergue, refreshments) and **Torres del Río** L (**26km**, 454m) (albergue, refreshments). Ascend steadily for 4km, winding through scrubland to summit (568m), then descend and ascend again before reaching beginning of **Viana** (**37.5km**, 460m) (accommodation, albergue, refreshments, tourist office).

To visit Viana, fork R at top of hill then turn R (Calle Conde San Cristóbal) through arch into walled city.

Fork R ahead uphill at roundabout (Calle la Solana) to pass through lower part of town. ◀ Follow road downhill to rejoin N-111 main road at roundabout and continue through vineyards to reach sign beside large paper mill R showing beginning of La Rioja region. ◀ Pass **Saicapack paper mill** R, then cross bridge over small river and immediately bear R onto asphalt cycle track parallel with road, joining camino route. Cycle under four road bridges and continue through vineyards with Monte Cantabria rising L. Cross main road and turn R on promenade beside río Ebro. Immediately before bridge, turn back R up ramp to road and L across Puente de Piedra bridge. Turn half-R at roundabout (Calle Ruavieja, cobbles, second exit), then go ahead over crossroads to reach Santiago church in old part of **Logroño** (**46km**, 382m) (accommodation, albergue, refreshments, camping, tourist office, cycle shop).

The N-111 has been renumbered NA-1110 in Navarre, but retains its N-111 number in La Rioja.

Modern pilgrim statue in Logroño

STAGE 5
Logroño to Santo Domingo de la Calzada

Start	Logroño, Santiago church (382m)
Finish	Santo Domingo de la Calzada cathedral (639m)
Distance	50km; road route 49.5km
Ascent	797m; road route 623m
Descent	540m; road route 366m

This is a stage of gently rolling treeless hills covered by vineyards that produce Rioja wine. The route climbs steadily out of Logroño through Navarrete to reach a rural summit at Alto de San Antón. It then drops into the río Nájerilla valley before rising again to cross a high ridge at a new golf course and residential development. It is mostly on well-surfaced gravel tracks with a few short rough sections. After following the camino route out of Logroño, the road route joins the N-120 which is followed to Santo Domingo.

Camino route
From Santiago church in **Logroño**, follow Calle de Barriocepo W. At end turn L and R (Calle de Marqués de San Nicolás) in front of Parliament of La Rioja and pass Puerta del Revellín gateway R. Turn L (Calle Once de Junio) and R (Calle Portales) out of old town. Go ahead over roundabout (Calle Marqués de Murrieta, third exit) and continue ahead over second roundabout. At third roundabout, turn L (Calle Duques de Nájera) past Guardia Civil barracks R using cycle track R. Turn R into small park and go ahead over railway bridge. Continue through Parque San Miguel and over road bridge. Pass pond R with wooden duck house in centre. Turn R at junction of tracks and at end of park bear R onto road. Go ahead over roundabout then turn immediately L across road at crossing point and bear R on brick-block track

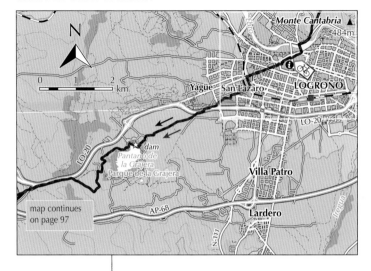

At this point the road route continues ahead on the N-120.

winding through parkland. Follow this bearing L under motorway and continue into open country. Cross bridge over side road, then fork L and turn R across **Pantano de la Grajera dam** (**5.5km**, 436m).

Immediately after dam, turn L along lakeside over wooden bridge then fork R uphill. Pass La Grajera bar L (refreshments) and continue on good-quality gravel track winding through open pine woodland. Pass transmission masts L and turn R at first T-junction onto asphalt track then L at second, ascending on road through vineyards. At top of hill, bear L at first parallel with motorway then bearing L beside N-120 main road. Where track ends, emerge on main road and continue ahead for 250 metres. ◄ Fork R on gravel track through vineyards, going ahead over N232, then forking L onto bridge over motorway. Pass ruins of San Juan de Acre pilgrim hospital and modern Don Jacobi bodega (both L), cycling through vineyards. Ascend, following road curving R and immediately turn sharply L, crossing main road. Fork R uphill (Calle Mayor Baja, cobbles) and fork R again (still Calle Mayor Baja) into **Navarrete** (**12.5km**, 513m) (accommodation, albergue, refreshments, camping, tourist office).

The foundation of **Navarrete** (pop 3000) is almost a mirror image of Viana, in that it was founded around a castle on Cerro Tedéon, built by the rulers of Castile to protect their territory from Navarre. No trace of the castle remains, but the streets contouring around the hill still follow the course of the old city walls. These streets contain many historic buildings including the Church of the Asunción with a stunning golden Plateresque *retablo* (altarpiece). The two main industries are pottery and wine. Clay from the slopes of Tedéon is used to make pitchers, jugs, mugs and crockpots by local potteries, some of which are open to visitors. The most characteristic piece is the Cántaro, a pitcher wider than it is tall, with a decorated border and a carrying handle that was used by local women to carry water on their heads. Navarrete is

The ruins of San Juan de Acre pilgrim hospital near Navarrete

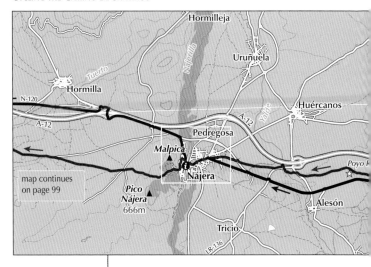

map continues
on page 99

an important town within the Rioja wine-producing denominación, with 11 bodegas producing mostly red wine.

Pass between tamarisk filled Plaza de las Pilas L and Church of the Asunción R and continue on Calle Mayor Alta. Cross Plaza del Arco with ornate drinking fountain in middle of road and turn L (Calle Arrabal) downhill. Continue on Calle San Roque and bear L on main road (N-120) out of town. Pass cemetery L and join gravel track

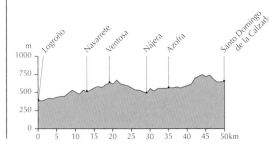

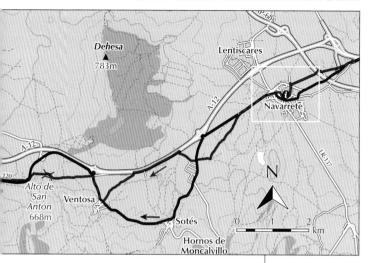

beside road L. After 300 metres, follow track bearing L away from road and ascending through vineyards. Turn R at staggered crossing of tracks, then continue across main road past bodega L. Descend to T-junction and turn R then L on gravel track parallel with motorway. Pass under two bridges and 300 metres after second bridge (pop-up refreshments), turn L on asphalt road ascending through vineyards to **Ventosa** (**19km**, 632m) (accommodation, albergue, refreshments). Turn R on main road and follow this downhill. Just before roundabout turn L on gravel track then fork R and ascend between vineyards over scrubby summit at **Alto de San Antón** (**21km**, 668m). ▶

The final part of the ascent is very steep and rocky for a short distance.

Descend past bodega L, then pass under main road and fork L parallel with road L. Follow track eventually moving R away from road, past transmission mast on **Poyo Roldán hilltop** L. ▶ Continue downhill past beehive-shaped shelter L and cross main road beside aggregates depot L. Fork L then turn L down steps with ramp for pushing cycles and cross bridge over río Yalde. Turn R along opposite bank then pass under road bridge. Immediately after pilgrim rest area L, turn sharply L past grain silo L and

Poyo Roldán hill was the site of a mythical fight to the death between Roland (who won) and Ferragut, a Saracen giant in the army of the Moors.

97

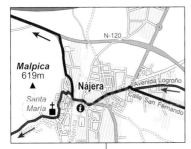

cross irrigation canal. Turn L across main road onto gravel track and continue on asphalt road (Ave Logroño). Bear R on main road and go ahead at roundabout (Calle San Fernando, second exit) into **Nájera** (**29km**, 485m) (accommodation, albergue, refreshments, camping, tourist office, cycle shop).

Originally a Roman settlement, **Nájera** (pop 8000) was developed by the Moors as a crossing point over the río Nájerilla (the name is Arabic for 'between cliffs'). After the Christian Reconquest (AD923) it became the capital of Navarre and remained a multi-cultural town with Christian, Jewish and Muslim communities. The monastery of Santa María la Real was founded in 1052 when King Garcia, while out hunting, 'discovered' a statue of the Virgin Mary in a cave lit by a lamp. He built a church by the cave, which developed into a powerful and rich monastery run by Benedictine monks

Santa María la Real monastery in Nájera

from the Order of Cluny until 1513, although nowadays it is managed by the Franciscans. The inside of the monastery church is highly decorated, especially the mausoleum of the Navarrean kings and the 15th-century wood-carved high choir. The cave where it all began is part of the church and can be visited.

Bear R following one-way system, then continue ahead on Puente de Piedra bridge over río Nájerilla. Turn R parallel with river then first L away from river beside house 2. Continue into Travesía la Estrella and bear L ahead through arch. Turn R (Calle Villegas) and turn L at end (Calle San Miguel). Continue past Plaza Santa María L into Calle de las Viudas, passing Santa María la Real monastery R. Follow road (Calle Costanilla) bearing R beside monastery, and ascend steeply out of town on gravel track through scrub and woodland to reach summit (552m). Continue undulating through vineyards, going ahead at crossing of paths and forking R at path junction. Emerge on road and follow this L through vineyards to **Azofra** (**35km**, 552m) (accommodation, albergue, refreshments).

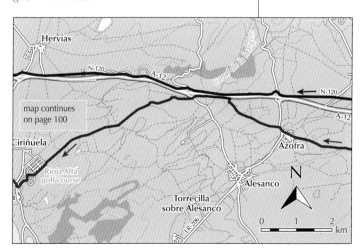

Fork R (Calle Mayor) through village centre. Bear R on main road to reach end of village then cross small bridge and fork L on quiet road through vineyards which soon becomes gravel track. Turn R at T-junction and after 100 metres, L parallel with motorway. Cross road beside motorway junction and fork L at junction of tracks. Turn L at T-junction and continue ascending steadily through fields and vineyards to reach road junction beside **Rioja Alta golf course**. Fork L, passing club house L (refreshments), then fork R at road junction. Turn L at crossroads, then go ahead over next crossroads and turn R after 50 metres (Calle el Monte). Pass through edge of **Cirueña** (**44.5km**, 743m) (albergue, refreshments) and turn R just before reaching main road.

Cross road using pedestrian crossing and turn R on opposite side. Bear L on gravel track beside roundabout and after 175 metres follow this bearing L away from road. Continue ahead through fields for 4.5km, descending steeply to reach road. Turn L, then go ahead over roundabout, crossing N-120. Fork R (Calle Doce de Mayo) and continue ahead over crossroads to

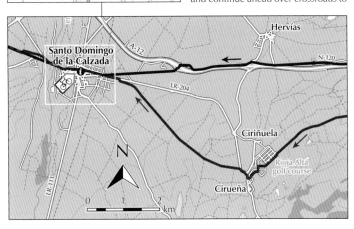

reach cathedral in **Santo Domingo de la Calzada** (**50km**, 639m) (accommodation, albergue, refreshments, tourist office, cycle shop).

SANTO DOMINGO DE LA CALZADA

The high altar in Santo Domingo cathedral

Santo Domingo de la Calzada (pop 6400) is a small city that grew as a result of the needs of pilgrims on the medieval Camino. In the late 11th century, a hermit Domingo García was granted land to build a church, hospital and bridge over the río Oja for the benefit by pilgrims. A small town grew up in what is now the Barrio Viejo. The cathedral was started in 1158, specifically to house the remains of Domingo who had died in 1109 and was subsequently canonised as Santo Domingo de la Calzada. The original building in late Romanesque style has been added to many times in a range of styles including Gothic, Mudéjar, Renaissance and Plateresque. The 69m Baroque tower was built in 1767 on a new site separate from the main church after a previous tower collapsed when a stream undermined its foundations. Inside the cathedral a cage holding a hen and a rooster represents a miracle of Santo Domingo who brought back to life a wrongly hanged boy and two chickens.

The rest of the town is a treasure house of old buildings, both spiritual and secular. These include the former San Francisco convent, nowadays a luxury parador hotel, and the Cistercian abbey, part of which is a pilgrim albergue.

Road route

From Santiago church in **Logroño**, follow Calle de Barriocepo W. At end turn L and R (Calle de Marqués de San Nicolás) in front of Parliament of La Rioja and pass Puerta del Revellín gateway R. Turn L (Calle Once de Junio) and R (Calle Portales) out of old town. Go ahead over roundabout (Calle Marqués de Murrieta, third exit) and continue ahead over second roundabout. At third roundabout, turn L (Calle Duques de Nájera) past Guardia Civil barracks R using cycle track R. Turn R into small park and go ahead over railway bridge. Continue through Parque San Miguel and over road bridge. Pass pond R with wooden duck house in centre. Turn R at junction of tracks and at end of park bear R onto road. Go ahead over roundabout then turn immediately L across road at crossing point and bear R on brick-block track winding through parkland. Follow this bearing L under motorway and continue into open country. Cross bridge over side road, then fork L and turn R across **Pantano de la Grajera dam** (**5.5km**, 436m).

Immediately after dam, turn L along lakeside over wooden bridge then fork R uphill. Pass La Grajera bar L (refreshments) and continue on good-quality gravel track winding through open pine woodland. Pass transmission masts L and turn R at first T-junction onto asphalt track then L at second, ascending on road through vineyards. At top of hill, bear L at first parallel with motorway then bearing L beside N-120 main road. Where track ends, emerge on N-120 and continue ahead passing point where camino route forks R on gravel track. Pass over

---

The road route has been made difficult by the conversion of the N-120 main road into a connecting road for the A-12 motorway with cycles prohibited. This affects the route in two places: leaving Logroño above the Grajera dam and passing Sotés, where no alternative surfaced roads have been provided. It is necessary to follow a good-quality gravel track for a short distance through Grajera country park while a rough gravel track can be followed past Sotés or a circuitous uphill detour on asphalt (described below) is available.

motorway, then fork L across road where N-120 swings R to bypass Navarrete. Follow road (Calle Abadía) passing through lower part of **Navarrete** with town centre on hillside R (**12.5km**, 505m) (accommodation, albergue, refreshments, camping, tourist office).

Turn L (Calle San Roque) and continue to reach N-120, then follow this out of town to roundabout at A-12 motorway junction. ▶ Take third exit (LR-342, sp Sotés) and follow road uphill past modern bodega R and through vineyards to **Sotés** (**17.5km**, 666m) (accommodation, refreshments).

A motorway has been constructed over the N-120 obliterating the route. You can either continue beside the motorway on a gravel track for 3km or take the route described uphill through Sotés.

In La Rioja the route passes through some of Spain's best vineyards

Turn R at T-junction (LR-341, sp Ventosa) and continue downhill past **Ventosa** L (**19.5km**, 632m) (accommodation, albergue, refreshments) to reach roundabout. Turn L (N-120, third exit, sp Huércanos) and follow this to outskirts of Nájera. Go ahead over roundabout, then after 600 metres fork L (Calle San Fernando, sp Nájera). Go ahead L at next roundabout (still Calle San Fernando) into centre of **Nájera** (**30km**, 485m) (accommodation, albergue, refreshments, camping, tourist office, cycle shop).

Bear R following one-way system, then continue ahead on Puente de Piedra bridge over río Nájerilla. Turn R parallel with river and continue out of town, with sheer red cliffs rising L, to reach N-120. Turn L (sp Burgos) and follow road ahead over roundabout (LR-313, second exit, sp Hormilla) to reach group of three roundabouts beside motorway junction. ◄ Turn R at first roundabout (second exit) over motorway then L at second (second exit). At third roundabout turn L again (second exit) past Valcarce motorway service area R (**33.5km**, 512m) (refreshments) to rejoin main road, now on opposite side of motorway. Continue beside motorway and pass next three motorway junctions. At fourth junction turn L (third exit, sp Santo Domingo) across motorway bridge. Go ahead over next roundabout (second exit, sp Santo Domingo) and follow road to roundabout on edge of Santo Domingo de le Calzada. Go ahead, then after 75 metres fork R (Calle Doce de Mayo) into centre of **Santo Domingo de la Calzada** (**49.5km**, 639m) (accommodation, albergue, refreshments, tourist office, cycle shop).

Follow signposts for N-120 Santo Domingo de la Calzada through all three roundabouts.

STAGE 6

*Santo Domingo de la Calzada to
Villafranca Montes de Oca*

Start	Santo Domingo de la Calzada cathedral (639m)
Finish	Villafranca Montes de Oca, Santiago church (944m)
Distance	34km; road route 33.5km
Ascent	579m; road route 540m
Descent	274m; road route 235m

This stage ascends steadily through open country, with undulations, to pass through the hilltop villages of Grañón and Viloria de Rioja before descending slightly to Belorado. After that it is steadily uphill to Villafranca in the foothills of the Montes de Oca. Part of the historic route has been lost under the asphalt of the A-12 motorway, with new tracks constructed to avoid this hazard. The road route mostly follows the N-120 with some deviations through villages beside the road.

Camino route

From cathedral in **Santo Domingo de la Calzada** follow Calle Mayor W. ▸ At end dogleg L and R (Calle río Palomarejos), then bear R on N-120 (Ave La Rioja). Cross río Oja and turn immediately R down ramp. At bottom turn sharply L onto track running parallel with but below main road. Turn R and L across LR-201 road onto gravel track past vehicle inspection depot L. Turn L at T-junction, then cross main road and turn R on track on opposite side of road. Go ahead over two track crossings then at third turn R and L to continue beside motorway. Dogleg R and L under edge of motorway to cross dual-level bridge over río Majuelos. Go ahead over staggered crossroads, ascending on asphalt road to reach beginning of **Grañón** (**6.5km**, 726m) (accommodation, albergue, refreshments).

Calle Mayor has several highly decorated houses built for rich noblemen.

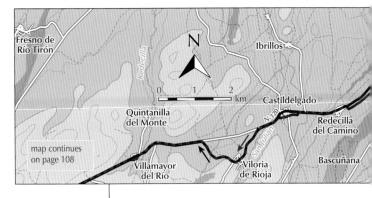

Cross road and bear L up ramp to avoid steps, then cycle ahead through village on Calle Mayor. Turn L at T-junction and after 40 metres, turn sharply R descending on quiet road between fields. Turn R at next junction, then after another 40 metres turn L. Go ahead over crossing of tracks, then turn L, uphill, at next junction. At crest pass large **Castilla y León sign** welcoming pilgrims to region. Descend steeply then continue through fields on concrete track to T-junction and turn R. Cross main road and bear L (Calle Mayor) through **Redecilla del Camino** (**10.5km**, 742m) (accommodation, albergue, refreshments, tourist office).

At end of village, dogleg R and L across main road onto gravel track parallel with road and cross río Reláchigo. Cycle along short asphalt section of old road, then continue on gravel track. Bear L away from road at next junction and follow road (Calle Mayor) through **Castildelgado** (**12km**, 769m) (accommodation, albergue,

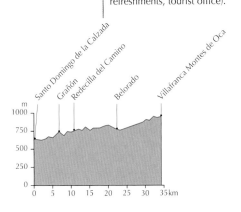

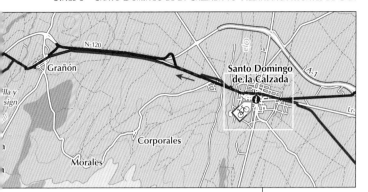

refreshments). At end of village, zigzag steeply downhill onto track beside main road. Cross río San Julián and continue to side road. Bear L uphill to **Viloria de Rioja** (**14km**, 800m) (accommodation, albergue, refreshments). ▶

Cycle through village on Calle Bajera, passing unusual half-timbered church L, then bear R downhill to T-junction. Turn L on gravel track beside main road and follow this to beginning of **Villamayor del Río** (**17.5km**,

Viloria de Rioja was the *cuna* (birthplace) of Santo Domingo and an old font in front of the church is claimed to be where he was baptised.

The Camino crosses the río Oja where Santo Domingo built his bridge in the 11th century

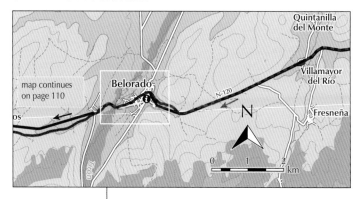

788m) (albergue, refreshments). Bear L away from road to pass through village, then return to track beside main road and follow this for 3.5km over low ridge. Eventually cross main road and bear R on gravel track descending into **Belorado** (**22km**, 769m) (accommodation, albergue, refreshments, tourist office, cycle shop).

The small leather producing town of **Belorado** (pop 2000) grew up around a 10th-century castle erected soon after the Christian Reconquest of northern Spain from the Moors, although little remains of this castle. The Monday market has been continuous since it was established by a 10th-century charter while the annual fiesta dates from another ancient charter (1116), making it the oldest in Spain. During the harvest thanksgiving festival in September, the men of the village partake in traditional group dances, accompanied by bagpipe-like instruments called *gaites*.

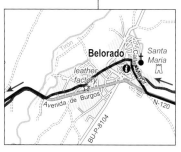

At beginning of built-up area, go ahead on cobbled Calle Corro and follow this as it bears L opposite Santa María church. Turn R at T-junction (Calle Mayor) then after 50 metres

turn L (Calle Raimundo de Miguel) and go ahead into Calle Hipólito López Bernal. Route becomes Ave Camino de Santiago, taking middle track at three-way fork and passing behind large *exposición piel* (leather showroom) L, then continues out of town.

Dogleg R and L across main road then bear R onto track behind derelict house and continue on bridge over río Tirón parallel with main road. Pass roundabout and continue on good-quality track through fields across valley to edge of **Tosantos** (**27km**, 821m) (albergue, refreshments). ▸

Pass village R on Calle Real and turn L to continue between fields to **Villambista** (**29km**, 860m) (albergue, refreshments). Fork L at beginning of village, then pass fountain R and go ahead on gravel track through fields. Emerge on main road, follow this L for 50 metres then fork R away from road to **Espinosa del Camino** (**30.5km**, 898m) (albergue, refreshments).

Go ahead (Calle Villafranca) winding through village and turn sharply L on gravel track into open country. Bear L at junction of tracks to reach N-120 main road and turn R on narrow track parallel with road. Follow

The ermita de la Virgen de la Peña chapel is cut into the hillside near Tosantos

Ermita de la Virgen de la Peña chapel, right, was built in the entrance to caves that held a statue of Christ for protection during the Moorish occupation.

109

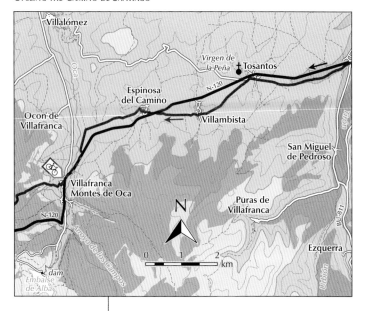

this over small bridge and continue to emerge in carpark. Bear L onto main road and continue to reach stage end at Santiago church in **Villafranca Montes de Oca** (**34km**, 944m) (accommodation, albergue, refreshments).

Road route

Leave **Santo Domingo de la Calzada** on N-120a (Ave La Rioja) and follow this for 2km. At point where road ahead becomes no entry, bear R over bridge and join N-120, heading W. ◄ Pass under two road bridges and 400 metres after second bridge turn L across road (sp Grañón) onto asphalt side road and follow this uphill to T-junction. Turn L and after 40 metres, bear R up ramp (avoiding steps) then cycle ahead on Calle Mayor through **Grañón** (**7km**, 726m) (accommodation, albergue, refreshments).

At end of village, turn L at T-junction and after 40 metres, turn sharply R descending on quiet road between fields. Turn R at next junction, then after

The route of the N-120 has been absorbed by an unfinished section of the A-12 motorway which blocks the road ahead. You can continue beside the road following the camino route on a gravel track or cycle on the road as described here.

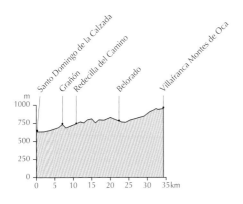

another 40 metres turn L. Go ahead over crossing of tracks and continue to reach main road. Turn L and follow N-120 ascending steadily to beginning of **Redecilla del Camino** (**11km**, 742m) (accommodation, albergue, refreshments, tourist office). Bear R to pass through village on Calle Mayor and rejoin main road after village. Continue through **Castildelgado** (**12.5km**, 764m) (accommodation, albergue, refreshments) and at crest of next hill, fork L (sp Viloria de Rioja) uphill to **Viloria de Rioja** (**14.5km**, 800m) (accommodation, albergue, refreshments).

Cycle through village on Calle Bajera, passing unusual half-timbered church L, then bear R downhill to T-junction. Turn L on N-120 and pass through **Villamayor del Río** (**17.5km**, 784m) (albergue, refreshments) to reach summit (**19km**, 826m), then descend into **Belorado** (**22.5km**, 771m) (accommodation, albergue, refreshments, tourist office, cycle shop).

Enter town on Ave de Logroño, then fork R after building number 1 (vehicle repair workshop) passing behind church and follow narrow Calle Mayor through town. Pass Santa María church set back R, then turn L (Calle Raimundo de Miguel) and go ahead into Calle Hipólito López Bernal. Route becomes Ave Camino de Santiago, taking middle track at three-way fork and

Villambista church and fountain

passing behind large *exposición piel* (leather showroom) L, then continues out of town.

Turn R on N-120, crossing río Tirón and go ahead over roundabout into open country. Ascend steadily through **Tosantos** (**27km**, 819m) (albergue, refreshments), then pass **Villambista** L (**29km**, 845m) (albergue, refreshments) and **Espinosa del Camino** R (**30.5km**, 898m) (albergue, refreshments) to reach stage end at Santiago church in **Villafranca Montes de Oca** (**33.5km**, 944m) (accommodation, albergue, refreshments).

STAGE 7
Villafranca Montes de Oca to Burgos

Start	Villafranca Montes de Oca, Santiago church (944m)
Finish	Burgos cathedral (857m)
Distance	38.5km; road route 36km
Ascent	406m; road route 292m
Descent	493m; road route 379m

This stage climbs steeply over the thickly forested Montes de Oca, an outlier of the Sierra de la Demanda, then descends into a small valley before a steep climb on rough tracks over the limestone Sierra de Atapuerca. Finally, the río Arlanzón is followed into El Cid's city of Burgos. The road route follows the N-120 over the mountains to the edge of Burgos. Both routes use segregated cycle tracks south of the river to reach the city centre.

Camino route

From Santiago church in **Villafranca Montes de Oca**, follow Cuesta del Hospital SW uphill, passing church L. Turn R, ignoring Camino waymarks pointing ahead on narrow walkers' path, and follow gravel track ascending steeply through forest. Pass Fuente de Mojapán R and bear R on broader track to reach **monument**. ▶ Cycle steeply downhill then cross small wooden bridge and go steeply up again to reach summit at 1158m. Descend steadily through forest, now on wide loggers' track and continue downhill past pop-up café (refreshments). Join good-quality gravel track that has come from Puerto de la Pedraja on N-120 road then fork L to reach tiny community of **San Juan de Ortega** (**12km**, 1004m) (albergue, refreshments).

The monument commemorates victims of the Spanish Civil War (1936–39).

The small hamlet of **San Juan de Ortega** sits beside an old monastery set in a remote location

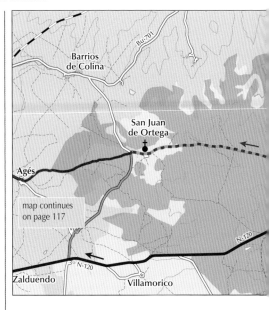

surrounded by forest. The monastery was built by
Juan de Ortega around 1142, specifically to provide
shelter for pilgrims making the hard crossing of the
Montes de Oca. When the pilgrimage declined, the
monastery fell into disrepair and was abandoned

*Monument to Spanish
Civil War victims near
Puerto de la Pedraja
in the Montes de Oca*

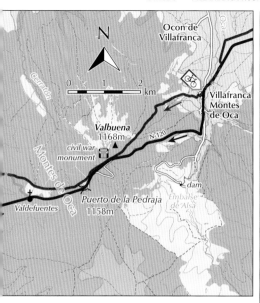

with the church used as a haybarn. The growth of the modern pilgrimage has led to gradual restoration, with the monastery now housing a 50-bed albergue and a café for pilgrims. The much photographed 12th-century church is in late Romanesque style with 15th-century additions. San Juan is buried in the crypt.

Pass church R and follow asphalt road for 300 metres. Pass road junction R on apex of bend and immediately after bend, turn R on gravel track resuming descent through forest. ▶ Emerge from forest and soon reach **Agés** (**15.5km**, 968m) (albergue, refreshments). Bear R onto road and follow this through **Atapuerca** (**18km**, 954m) (albergue, refreshments).

Just before end of village, turn L on gravel track beside monument to pre-hominid ancestors. After 600 metres, fork R, ascending steeply on rocky track with

The route over Alto de Atapuerca is steep and rocky. It can be bypassed by turning left at the road junction here on the bend (sp Santovenia de Oca) to join the road route on the N-120.

115

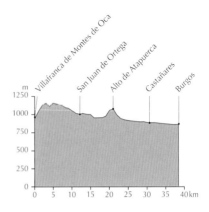

coiled barbed wire fence of military area L, to reach summit cross at **Alto de Atapuerca** (**20.5km**, 1076m).

The limestone ridge of the **Sierra de Atapuerca** is riddled with karst-system caves which for nearly one million years have been used as shelter by animals and humans. When mining to provide coal,

Descending from Atapuerca towards Burgos

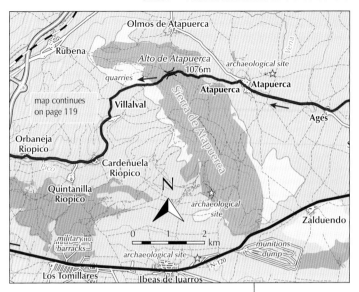

iron ore and limestone for steelworks around Bilbao commenced during the late 19th century, a railway was built to access the mines which involved digging a deep cutting through the hillside. This opened up previously unknown cave systems revealing pre-hominid remains and human bones dating back before the Stone Age. Archaeological excavations are on-going and the site has been accorded UNESCO world heritage status. Many of the finds are displayed in the Museo de la Evolución Humana in Burgos.

Continue ahead across summit plateau then follow rough track downhill into río Pico valley with military fence L and Burgos visible ahead. Go ahead at first track junction then bear L at T-junction. Turn L downhill at next junction (sp Burgos) to reach asphalt road and bear R. Cycle through **Cardeñuela Ríopico** (**24km**, 923m) (albergue, refreshments) and continue to **Orbaneja Ríopico**

117

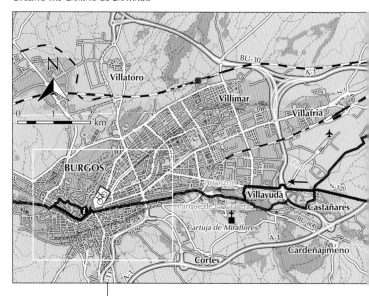

(**26.5km**, 909m) (albergue, refreshments). Follow road over motorway and after 250 metres turn L passing housing development R. ◄ Follow gravel track to perimeter of **Burgos airport** and turn L, following perimeter fence R for 1.75km. Follow fence round bend R then where fence turns R again, continue ahead past red and white electricity pylon R to reach N-120 main road in **Castañares** (**31km**, 885m) (accommodation, refreshments).

The left turn is poorly signed and easy to miss.

Cross main road and go ahead (Calle Óbidos) through housing estate then bear R in front of aggregate depot gates. Where road ends, continue on track and bear L crossing bridge over río Arlanzón. Fork L and follow concrete track, bearing R parallel with motorway. Turn L following gravel track under motorway then bear L winding through woodland. ◄ At fork of tracks, bear L again to reach road. Turn R, then R again onto main road. Follow this for 350 metres, then turn R opposite pedestrian crossing passing through wooden rail fence onto asphalt cycle track. Fork L, winding through

Ignore the yellow arrows pointing right along a rough track.

woodland, then bear L parallel with river R. ▶

Continue through Parque de Fuentes Blancas (camping) and pass under road bridge. Immediately after bridge, join red asphalt cycle track L and follow this winding through wooded parkland. Cross park road and bear R following cycle track beside this road. Pass under road bridge, then just after third roundabout follow cycle track across road and continue on other side, passing modern Museo de la Evolución Humana L. Pass beside pedestrian and road bridges over river R, then turn R across second pedestrian bridge (Puente Santa María). Go ahead through arch (Arco de Santa María) to reach stage end in square on S side of the cathedral in **Burgos** (**38.5km**, 857m) (accommodation, albergue, refreshments, tourist office, cycle shop, station).

The road route joins here.

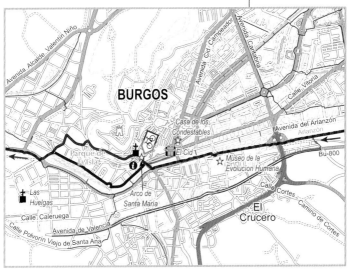

119

BURGOS

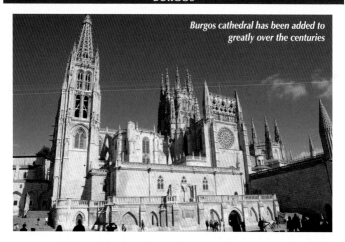

Burgos cathedral has been added to greatly over the centuries

The castle at Burgos (pop 177,000), perched on a hilltop overlooking the Arlanzón valley, was built (AD884) soon after the Christian reconquest of northern Spain. A few houses below the castle developed into a town which became the capital of Castile from 1038 to 1085. The town's most famous son, Rodrigo Díaz de Vivar (circa 1040–99), better known as 'El Cid', was a military leader who participated in the Reconquest. However, he fell out with his regal and political masters and became a mercenary general fighting battles for whoever paid the most, be they Christian or Moor. He ended up capturing and ruling his own state, Valencia, although after his death his body was brought back to Burgos and he was buried in the cathedral.

The growth of the pilgrimage brought wealth and prosperity to Burgos, particularly as it also sat on the main north–south trade route between central Spain and the French border at Irun. Many religious buildings were constructed, including the great Gothic cathedral. The huge Cistercian monastery of Santa María la Real de las Huelgas (1189) holds the mausoleum of the royalty and nobility of Castile while the Cartuja de Miraflores Carthusian monastery (1453) is considered one of the finest late Gothic buildings in the country. The Plateresque hospital del Rey has been restored and now houses the law faculty of Burgos university. The medieval city was surrounded by 4km of walls with 90 towers and 12 gates. Parts of these remain with the

Arco de Santa María gateway the best preserved. Within the city, the Casa de los Condestables was the location of a meeting between Christopher Columbus and the Spanish monarchs when he returned from his second voyage to America.

The first half of the 16th century was the peak of prosperity for medieval Burgos, with its population reaching 25,000. However, with reduction in the pilgrimage, the city went into a prolonged period of economic decline and the population fell to 4500 by 1600. This depression continued until the railway arrived in 1860 bringing industrialisation. During the Civil War, Burgos was a nationalist stronghold and General Franco's headquarters from 1936–39. Post-war growth has been strong, particularly since 1970, and the city now has a broad industrial and commercial sector with many new buildings and wide boulevards. With 60km of dedicated cycle tracks, Burgos has the best provision in Spain in terms of kilometres per head and the second highest cycle use as a percentage of all journeys.

Road route

From Santiago church in **Villafranca Montes de Oca**, follow N-120 main road S through village into forest, soon curving R and climbing steeply to reach **Puerto de la Pedraja** (**4km**, 1150m). Continue climbing through forest to reach summit (1158m) then descend past **ermita de Valdefuentes chapel** R (**6.5km**, 1106m). ▶ Continue downhill through **Zalduendo** (**16.5km**, 994m)

A right turn into the forest beside the chapel links with the camino route and leads to San Juan de Ortega; a return route rejoins before Zalduendo.

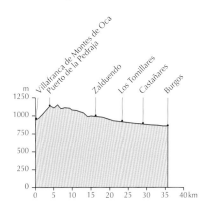

121

(refreshments), **Ibeas de Juarros** (**21km**, 933m) (refreshments) and **Los Tomillares** (**23.5km**, 915m) (accommodation, refreshments) then go under motorway and pass through **Castañares** (**29km**, 885m) (accommodation, refreshments).

Continue ahead at roundabout under motorway junction and past factories R. At first pedestrian crossing (opposite El Moreno bar R), turn L across dual carriageway into Plaza Vista Alegre in San Vicente (**31km**, 875m). Dogleg R and L between houses and continue ahead over series of crossroads. Cross río Arlanzón and turn R to join red asphalt cycle track beside river. Continue through Parque de Fuentes Blancas (camping) and pass under road bridge. Immediately after bridge, join red asphalt cycle track L and follow this winding through wooded parkland. Cross park road and bear R following cycle track beside this road. Pass under road bridge, then just after third roundabout follow cycle track across road and continue on other side, passing modern Museo de la Evolución Humana L. Pass beside pedestrian and road bridges over river R, then turn R across second pedestrian bridge (Puente Santa María). Go ahead through arch (Arco de Santa María) to reach stage end in square on S side of cathedral in **Burgos** (**36km**, 857m) (accommodation, albergue, refreshments, tourist office, cycle shop, station).

Burgos castle was built in AD884 soon after the Christian reconquest of the city

STAGE 8
Burgos to Castrojeriz

Start	Burgos cathedral (857m)
Finish	Castrojeriz, Plaza Mayor (816m)
Distance	40km; road route 51.5km
Ascent	327m; road route 376m
Descent	368m; road route 417m

After negotiating the streets of Burgos and a series of new tracks that avoid motorway junctions and high-speed railway lines, this route reaches the meseta, a dominant geographic feature of central Spain. Field tracks are followed undulating over three limestone downland ridges planted with endless fields of wheat and sunflowers. There is no human habitation save for two small villages in the folds of the downs. Equally, there is no shade, so take a good supply of water. The road route makes a long detour to the north, but still climbs over three ridges.

Camino route

From NW corner of cathedral in **Burgos**, follow cobbled Calle Fernán González SW past Meson del Cid hotel L and monumental arch of Fernán González R. Continue downhill on asphalt through Arco San Martin gateway. After 75 metres, turn L across main road steeply down-hill into street opposite and at staggered crossroads turn R (Calle Emperador). After 250 metres, turn sharply L (Calle Villalón), then go ahead over angled crossroads to reach T-junction. Cross road into gardens and con-tinue on bridge over río Arlanzón. Cross main road and turn R on red asphalt cycle track. Follow this past three roundabouts and university of Burgos L, which contains the restored ruins of the hospital del Rey. Just before road curves L, cross road R before bus shelter then turn L and fork R (Calle Benito Pérez Galdós, sp Los Guindales) past **Barriada del Pilar** L (**3km**, 843m). ▶

The road route continues ahead on a cycle track beside the main road.

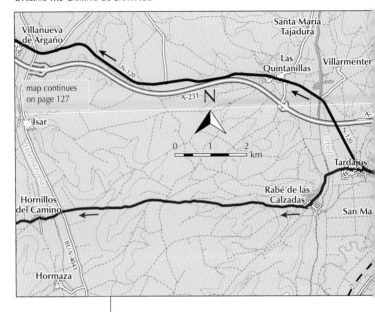

Where road ends, continue ahead on gravel track through open country, passing prison visible behind fields R. At mini-roundabout, turn R and immediately L to continue on track between fields. Turn R under railway bridge and L beside railway. Continue through fields to crossing of tracks and turn R over motorway. Turn sharply L at T-junction then bear R beside motorway and pass under bridge. Bear R and L to pass under second motorway bridge and reach N-120 main road. Bear R on path L and continue to **Tardajos** (**10.5km**, 827m) (albergue, refreshments).

Fork L into village (Calle del Mediodía) then turn R and fork L (Calle Real) to reach Plaza Leandro Mayoral with tree-shaded fountain in centre. Continue into Calle Real Poniente, passing church R and winding through village into open country. Cross río Urbel and follow quiet road into **Rabé de las Calzadas** (**12.5km**, 829m) (accommodation, albergue, refreshments).

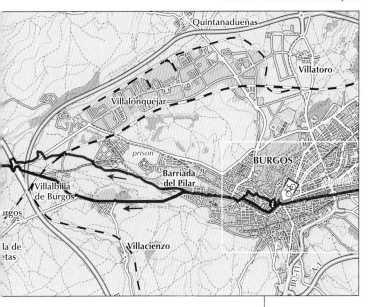

Ermita de Nuestra Señora chapel in Rabé de las Calzadas

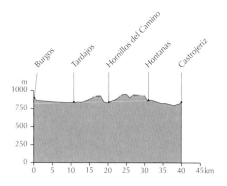

Turn R in village (Calle Santa Marina), to reach Plaza Francisco Riberas with fountain in centre. Continue past church L, then turn R (Calle Baldomero Pampliega) and follow this out of village, passing ermita de Nuestra Señora chapel L. Fork L at track junction and follow gravel track ascending steadily across open chalk downland to reach summit (922m). Descend crossing country road and follow asphalt road into **Hornillos del Camino** (**20.5km**, 824m) (albergue, refreshments).

Cycle through village then pass weighbridge R and fork R on gravel track. After 600 metres fork L, ascending through fields back onto downland to reach another summit (937m). Drop down into and climb out of small valley then continue across plateau. Cross small road then start descending, with village visible below. Fork R taking middle of three tracks and descend steeply around bends into **Hontanas** (**31km**, 878m) (accommodation, albergue, refreshments).

The track becomes very muddy when wet; the road can be used as an alternative.

Continue downhill through village and bear R at road junction. Go ahead across next road junction and bear L on vehicular track opposite. After 300 metres, turn L on gravel track and follow this gently downhill along valley for 3km. ◄ Emerge on road and turn R passing ruins of **San Antón monastery** L (albergue, refreshments).

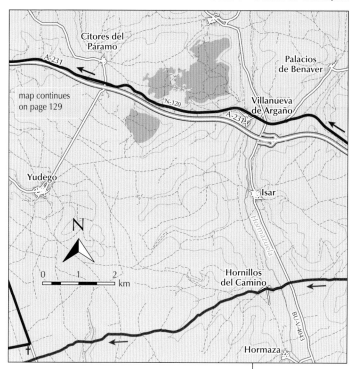

The ruined **pilgrim hospital** at the monastery of San Antón specialised in treating pilgrims with a disease known as St Anthony's fire or ergotism. Medieval doctors would prescribe sufferers to make the pilgrimage and they would journey to Castrojeriz seeking a cure, which appeared to work. At the time, this was claimed to be a miracle, but modern-day medicine provides a more prosaic explanation. Ergotism is caused by elevated levels of lysergic acid in the body usually the result of consuming products made with mouldy rye flour. The monastery treated patients by serving bread made only

from fresh wheat flour, hence the
disease was 'cured'.

Continue along road to reach
beginning of Castrojeriz. Fork R off
main road, then R again passing Santa
María del Manzano church R. Follow
road (Ave de la Colegiata) bearing L.
Turn first R (Ave de la Colegiata) uphill,
then bear L at top of hill and follow
Calle Real de Oriente passing bars
and albergues to reach arcaded Plaza Mayor in centre
of **Castrojeriz** (**40km**, 816m) (accommodation, albergue,
refreshments, camping, tourist office).

Castrojeriz (pop 800) is spread along the side of an
isolated rocky outcrop overlooking the confluence
of the Odra and Pisuerga rivers. Celtic, Roman and
Visigoth camps all topped the hill before a 10th-
century castle was built during the Reconquista.

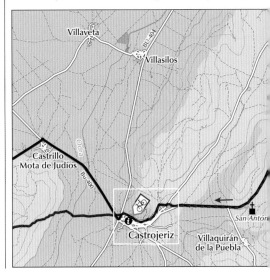

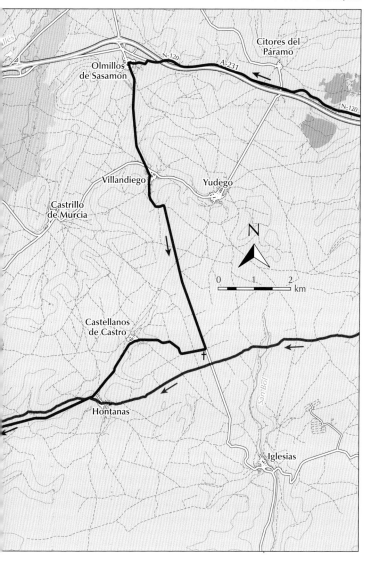

The ruins of Castrojeriz castle on a hilltop above Santa María de Manzano church

The village below is 1500 metres long but only 150 metres wide with the Camino following the main street for the length of the village and passing a number of churches and old pilgrim hospitals.

Road route

Start from square on SE side of cathedral in **Burgos** and retrace route through Arco de Santa María gateway. Turn R (Paseo de la Audiencia) and continue parallel with río Arlanzón L. Go ahead over roundabout (Paseo de la Isla, second exit) on red asphalt cycle track behind low hedge L of road. Where this ends, bear L on stone bridge over river then cross main road and turn R on red asphalt cycle track beside Paseo de la Universidad. Follow this past three roundabouts and university of Burgos L into **Barriada del Pilar** (**3km**, 843m). Where cycle track ends, continue on N-120 main road, going ahead over two roundabouts and passing **Villalbilla de Burgos** (**7km**, 839m) (accommodation, refreshments). Pass over railway and under motorway bridges to reach roundabout under motorway junction. Turn L (N-120, third exit, sp Tardajos) and continue to **Tardajos** (**10km**, 827m) (albergue, refreshments).

Keep ahead in village, then pass under motorway and continue to **Las Quintanillas** (**14km**, 844m). After village, road ascends steadily onto chalk downland to summit (925m), then descends into **Villanueva de Argaño** (**21.5km**, 839m) (accommodation, refreshments). Climb steady to another summit (936m) and then follow steep descent. Pass under motorway, then turn L at next junction into **Olmillos de Sasamón** (**30.5km**, 829m) (accommodation, refreshments).

Turn L (Calle Real) opposite church in village centre and follow road past **Villandiego** L (**33.5km**, 864m), climbing steeply onto top of plateau (933m). Cycle across plateau for 5km, passing windfarm R, then turn R by pilgrim cross (sp Castrojeriz). Descend steadily past **Castellanos de Castro** R (**41km**, 884m) then continue gently downhill on tree-lined road along floor of narrow valley with limestone cliffs rising on both sides. Pass ruins of **San Antón monastery** L (albergue, refreshments) to reach beginning of Castrojeriz. Fork R off main road, then R again passing Santa María del Manzano church R. Follow road (Ave de la Colegiata) bearing L. Turn first R (Ave de la Colegiata) uphill, then bear L at top of hill and follow Calle Real de Oriente passing bars and albergues to reach arcaded Plaza Mayor in centre of **Castrojeriz** (**51.5km**, 816m) (accommodation, albergue, refreshments, camping, tourist office).

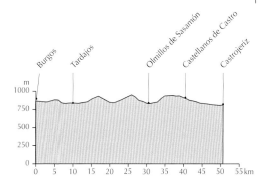

131

STAGE 9

Castrojeriz to
Carrión de los Condes

Start	Castrojeriz, Plaza Mayor (816m)
Finish	Carrión de los Condes, Santiago church (838m)
Distance	43.5km; road route 45km
Ascent	323m; road route 232m
Descent	301m; road route 210m

This stage continues across the open agricultural country of the meseta, although it is less exposed than the previous stage. A short steep climb is followed by undulating field paths and a canal towpath that leads to Frómista. The remainder of the stage is on a boringly straight senda beside a main road ascending gently to Carrión de los Condes. The road route first follows quiet country roads across the meseta, often some distance from the Camino, rejoining it at Frómista.

Camino route

From Plaza Mayor in **Castrojeriz**, follow Calle Real de Poniente NW, passing parish church of San Juan L. Bear L and fork R over crossroads then continue on track across main road descending through fields. Fork L to cross río Odra by seasonal **ford**. ◄ Ascend steeply (12 per cent) up bare limestone hillside to reach summit at **Alto Mostelares** (**3.5km**, 913m). Descend even more steeply (18 per cent) on concrete track through fields to reach quiet road and bear R. After 800 metres turn L, descending through fields. Pass ancient pilgrim hospital of **San Nicolás Puentefitero** L (albergue) and cross bridge over río Pisuerga. Bear R on track beside river, continuing to crossroads and go ahead (Calle Juan Jose Lopez) into **Itero de la Vega** (**11km**, 773m) (accommodation, albergue, refreshments).

The ford is usually dry in summer. If the river is high, fork right to use the walkers' track crossing the river on a narrow wooden bridge.

Turn L (Calle Eusebio Ibañez) and fork R (Calle Santa Ana) through village, then continue on asphalt road through fields to reach crossroads. Go ahead on gravel track crossing irrigation canal and climbing over low

Leaving Castrojeriz, the Camino climbs steeply over the Alto de Mostelares

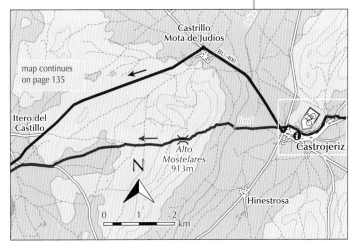

map continues on page 135

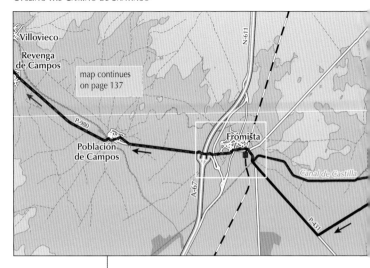

ridge, then descending to **Boadilla del Camino** (**19km**, 783m) (accommodation, albergue, refreshments).

Fork L and turn R to reach Plaza Mayor, then turn R (Calle Mayor) and continue out of village. After 300 metres, turn L beside barn and follow track through fields to reach **Canal de Castilla**.

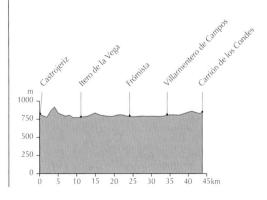

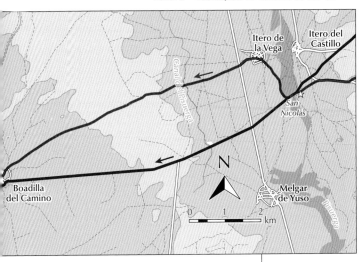

The 207km-long **Canal de Castilla** was part of a much larger (400km) 18th-century project to open trade links between central Spain and the north

Canal de Castilla, nowadays un-navigable, is used to supply irrigation water

135

coast port of Santander. It took 100 years to build half the total distance and the difficult part through the Cantabrian mountains to the Atlantic never materialised. The canal had its heyday between 1850–70, when 400 horse-drawn barges plied their trade. Business subsequently declined due to competition from the railways and the canal was abandoned as a transport system in the 20th century. It has, however, been retained as part of an irrigation network that brings water from the mountains to the plains of central Spain.

The road route joins here.

Turn L along towpath alongside canal, then cycle downhill beside Frómista locks to reach road. ◄ Turn R

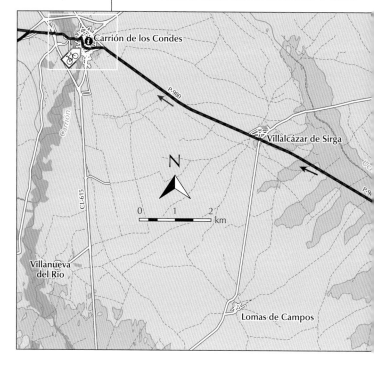

across canal then bear R and L and continue under railway bridge to reach crossroads with main road in **Frómista** (**24.5km**, 781m) (accommodation, albergue, refreshments, tourist office, station).

The golden age of **Frómista** (pop 800) was between the 11th and 15th centuries when it had a population of 4500. As a promi-nent place on the Camino, it had highly deco-rated churches, monasteries and pilgrim hospitals. San Martin's church is one of the most complete Romanesque churches in Europe and is well known for its stone-carved decoration. Santa María and San Pedro churches are both Gothic with Renaissance additions. The decline of the pilgrimage led to a long depression in Frómista's fortunes. Population fell to 217 and did not grow until the arrival of the canal and railways in the 19th century which brought a brief period of prosperity for 1500 people. Over the past 150 years the population has fallen again and, like many towns and villages in the region, continues to decline.

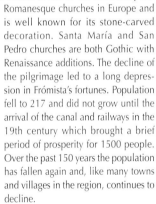

Go ahead over crossroads and bear L (Paseo Julio Senador, P980). Continue over two roundabouts (part of motorway junction) and join track beside main road. ▶ After 2km bear R to follow side road through **Población de Campos** (**28.5km**, 777m) (accommodation, albergue, refreshments). Bear L (Calle Escuelas) in village and return to main road. Bear R, then turn L over río

This is your first long stretch of senda (roadside track). If the road is quiet and the senda busy with walkers, you are better off cycling on the road.

137

Ucieza and continue beside main road through **Revenga de Campos** (**32km**, 787m), **Villarmentero de Campos** (**34km**, 789m) (accommodation, albergue, refreshments) and **Villalcázar de Sirga** (**38km**, 802m) (accommodation, albergue, refreshments).

Ascend over small ridge to reach beginning of Carrión de los Condes. Turn L beside grain silo (Ave de los Peregrinos) then go ahead over crossroads into Calle de Santa María and follow this to reach Santiago church R in centre of **Carrión de los Condes** (**43.5km**, 838m) (accommodation, albergue, refreshments, camping, tourist office, cycle shop).

The former San Zoilo monastery in Carrión de los Condes is now a luxury hotel

Carrión de los Condes (pop 2150) is another town that prospered from the pilgrimage. San Zoilo Benedictine monastery, a bridge over río Carrión and a pilgrim hospital were all built in the 11th century. Other buildings followed including Santiago church, where the representation of Christ in Majesty on the front wall is a renowned work of Romanesque stone sculpture, and Santa María church. By the 12th century the town was described

in the Codex Calixtinus as 'rich in bread and wine'. As a local religious and administrative centre, the town survived the decline in the pilgrimage better than others and in the 18th century was raised to the status of a city, albeit a small one.

Road route

From Plaza Mayor in **Castrojeriz**, follow Calle Real de Poniente NW, passing parish church of San Juan L. Bear L, then turn L at crossroads to reach roundabout. Turn R (first exit, BU-400, sp Castrillo Mota de Judíos) and follow main road over río Odra and past **Castrillo Mota de Judíos** (**4km**, 786m). Turn L at roundabout (sp Itero, BU-403) and continue across open downland, ignoring turn R to Itero del Castillo, to reach and cross bridge over río Pisuerga (**11km**, 766m). ▶ Continue to **Boadilla de la Camino** (**19.5km**, 782m) (accommodation, albergue, refreshments).

Go ahead through edge of village on Calle Abilio Calderón and continue through open country to T-junction. Turn R and follow road over Canal de Castilla and under railway bridge to reach crossroads in **Frómista** (**26km**, 781m) (accommodation, albergue, refreshments, tourist office, station).

Go ahead over crossroads and bear L (Paseo Julio Senador, P980). Continue over two roundabouts (part of motorway junction) into open country. After 2km bear R to follow side road through **Población**

The río Pisuerga bridge is also used by the camino route.

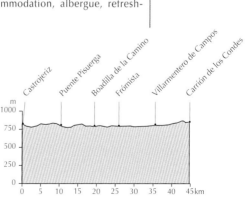

San Martin's in Frómista is the most perfect Romanesque church on the Camino

de Campos (**28.5km**, 777m) (accommodation, albergue, refreshments). Bear L (Calle Escuelas) in village and return to main road. Bear R, then turn L over río Ucieza and continue through **Revenga de Campos** (**33.5km**, 787m), **Villarmentero de Campos** (**35.5km**, 789m) (accommodation, albergue, refreshments) and **Villalcázar de Sirga** (**39.5km**, 802m) (accommodation, albergue, refreshments).

Ascend over small ridge to reach beginning of Carrión de los Condes. Turn L beside grain silo (Ave de los Peregrinos) then go ahead over crossroads into Calle de Santa María and follow this to reach Santiago church R in centre of **Carrión de los Condes** (**45km**, 838m) (accommodation, albergue, refreshments, camping, tourist office, cycle shop).

STAGE 10

Carrión de los Condes to Sahagún

Start	Carrión de los Condes, Santiago church (838m)
Finish	Sahagún, Trinidad church (835m)
Distance	39km; road route 42km
Ascent	216m; road route 233m
Descent	219m; road route 236m

This gently undulating stage follows gravel roads and sendas across the meseta. Villages are widely spaced and there is no shade. The road route alternative follows the N-120 throughout.

Camino route

From Santiago church in **Carrión de los Condes**, follow Calle Esteban Collantes N to reach crossroads. Turn L (Calle Piña Blasco) and continue over río Carrión into Calle San Zoilo. Pass San Zoilo monastery L then go ahead over roundabout (second exit, sp Calzada N-120) to reach junction with N-120. ▶ Cross main road and

The road route turns left along the N-120.

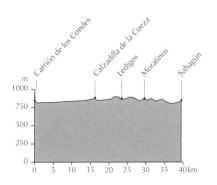

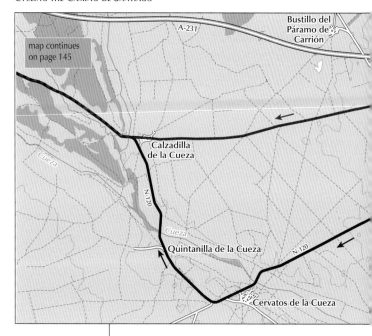

follow quiet road ahead for 3.5km to T-junction. Continue straight ahead on gravel road along route of old Roman road gently ascending through wheat fields to **Calzadilla de la Cueza** (**17km**, 857m) (accommodation, albergue, refreshments).

Follow Calle Mayor descending through village and bear R on N-120 main road. After 125 metres, join gravel senda L of road, rising gently at first then climbing and descending over low ridge. At bottom of descent, fork R on side road to reach edge of **Ledigos** (**23km**, 873m) (accommodation, albergue, refreshments). Turn L (Calle Ronda de Abajo) and continue ahead towards N-120. Just before main road, turn R then bear R following old route of main road past village. At end of village turn L across main road and continue on gravel senda on other side. Cross río Cueza and continue beside road. Bear L on

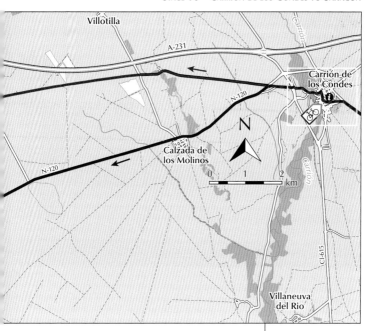

concrete track into **Terradillos de los Templarios** (**26km**, 877m) (albergue, refreshments).

Fork L, passing red-brick church R, then turn L at T-junction. Follow road round sharp bend R and after 25 metres turn L. Go ahead across staggered crossroads gently downhill out of village on gravel track to reach road. Turn L along road and after 400 metres, turn R on gravel track through fields, ascending gently to **Moratinos** (**29.5km**, 860m) (accommodation, albergue, refreshments). Turn R at beginning of village on concrete track, then bear L, passing church L and go ahead over crossroads. Fork R on gravel road winding over low ridge then descending to **San Nicolás del Real Camino** (**32km**, 847m) (albergue, refreshments).

At beginning of village, turn L at crossroads (Calle la Era) past church L and continue ahead through village.

Ermita de la Virgin del Puente chapel and the two pillars which mark the half-way point

Cross río Sequillo then turn R at crossing of tracks to reach N-120 main road. Turn L on senda L of road climbing gently to motorway junction. Follow track turning

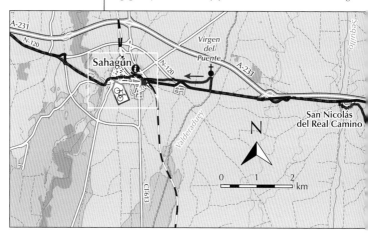

R away from main road then bear R beside motorway slip road to rejoin main road and continue downhill on senda to cross río Valderaduey. Turn R on track beside river, then turn L beside **ermita de la Virgen del Puente chapel**. ▸

Continue under Sahagún bypass, then go ahead across main road into Calle Ronda Estación. Bear R, parallel with railway past bullring R, then turn L over railway bridge. Turn second R (Calle del Arco) to reach redbrick former Trinidad church R in **Sahagún** (**39km**, 835m) (accommodation, albergue, refreshments, camping, tourist office, cycle shop, station) which nowadays houses the tourist office.

Two pillars just after the chapel mark the 'official' half-way point of the Camino between Roncesvalles and Santiago.

Sahagún (pop 2650) developed around the burial site of second-century Christian martyrs Fecundo and Primitivo. In the 11th century the royal monastery of San Benito was established by King Alfonso VI to preserve the martyrs' relics. This was given to the Benedictine order of monks from Cluny and grew to

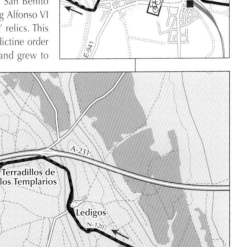

The Arco de San Benito gateway is a copy of the original entrance to San Benito monastery

become, for 400 years, one of the leading religious houses in Spain. Decline began in the 15th century when power moved to Valladolid and was completed when the monastery was suppressed in 1820. Only one clocktower (there were two), part of the abbey church and a few ruins remain. The Arco de San Benito gateway, said to be the original entrance to the abbey, is a copy constructed in 1662. Other significant buildings include the brick-built parish church of San Lorenzo and the church of San Tirso, both in Romanesque/Mudéjar style.

Road route

From Santiago church in **Carrión de los Condes**, follow Calle Esteban Collantes N to reach crossroads. Turn L (Calle Piña Blasco) and continue over río Carrión into Calle San Zoilo. Pass San Zoilo monastery L then go ahead over roundabout (second exit, sp Calzada N-120) to reach junction with N-120 and turn L. Follow this past **Calzada de los Molinos** L (**4.5km**, 825m) then cross río Cueza and continue past **Cervatos de la Cueza** L (**15.5km**, 855m). **Quintanilla de la Cueza** R (**18km**, 848m) and **Calzadilla de la Cueza** R (**21km**, 853m) (accommodation, albergue, refreshments).

Road now rises gently then ascends and descends over low ridge past **Ledigos** R (**27km**, 873m) (accommodation, albergue, refreshments). Follow gently undulating road as it bears L to run parallel with A-231 motorway, continuing past **Terradillos de los Templarios** L (**30km**, 892m) (albergue, refreshments), **Moratinos** L (**33.5km**, 867m) (accommodation, albergue, refreshments) and **San Nicolás del Real Camino** L (**35.5km**, 847m) (albergue, refreshments). Cross río Sequillo, then pass motorway junction R and continue over río Valderaduey to reach road junction on outskirts of Sahagún. Fork R, then follow slip road back under main road. Bear R at roundabout (first exit), then at next crossroads turn L (Calle Ronda Estación). Bear R, parallel with railway past bullring R, then turn L over railway bridge. Turn second R (Calle del Arco) to reach red-brick former Trinidad church R in **Sahagún** (**42km**, 835m) (accommodation, albergue, refreshments, camping, tourist office, cycle shop, station) which nowadays houses the tourist office.

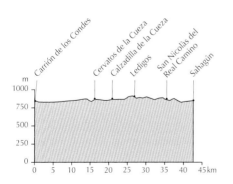

STAGE 11
Sahagún to León

Start	Sahagún, former Trinidad church (835m)
Finish	León cathedral (840m)
Distance	55km; road route 54.5km
Ascent	258m; road route 253m
Descent	253m; road route 248m

This stage, continuing across the meseta, previously started with a long dusty crossing of a remote treeless plateau; but things have changed a lot. The 21km track from Bercianos to Mansilla de las Mulas now has shade trees planted along its entire length, a motorway and high-speed railway line to keep you company and a network of irrigation canals that bring water down from the Cantabrian mountains. After coming off the plateau, a main road is followed over a low ridge before descending through the suburbs of León. With a few short variations, the road route closely follows the camino route.

Camino route
From Trinidad church in **Sahagún**, cycle E and turn L (Calle la Herrería) to reach crossroads. Turn R and fork immediately L (Calle Antonio Nicolás). Pass Santa Cruz monastery R and continue past Arco de San Benito gateway (visible 100 metres R along first side street), out of town. Bear R over río Cea on Puente Canto bridge and continue ahead past campsite R using tree-lined senda L of road. Go straight ahead at roundabout, by turning L across first exit and following track L beside second exit, to reach N-120 main road. Continue on senda L of road for 2km, then cross road and continue on other side for short distance. Cross side road that leads across motorway to **Calzada del Coto** (1km away R) and fork immediately R on gravel track. Continue ahead onto tree-lined gravel senda beside asphalt road parallel with motorway

R, following this under high-speed railway line. Continue over irrigation canal gently uphill to reach **Bercianos del Real Camino** (**10.5km**, 857m) (albergue, refreshments).

Follow Calle Mayor ahead through village, curving R in centre. After village, regain shaded senda and follow this ahead ascending gently through fields. Pass under motorway and railway to reach edge of **El Burgo Ranero**

From Sahagún to Mansilla de las Mulas the Camino follows shaded sendas beside a quiet country road

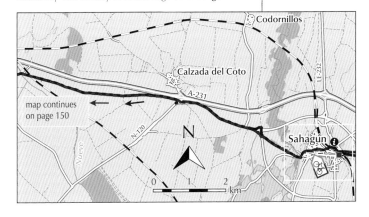

map continues on page 150

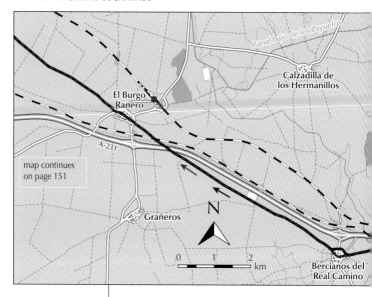

(**17.5km**, 880m) (accommodation, albergue, refreshments, station).

Dogleg R and L to follow Calle Real through centre of village. After village, rejoin senda and follow this through fields. Pass turn-off for Villamarco (**25.5km**,

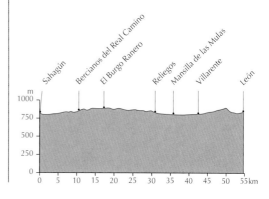

864m), then cross Canal alto de los Payuelos irrigation canal and pass under railway. Continue winding through fields, descending gently to **Reliegos** (**30.5km**, 825m) (albergue, refreshments). Fork L (Calle Real) through village then continue on senda crossing motorway. At end of shaded senda, fork L to cross bridge over Mansilla de las Mulas bypass. Follow road over irrigation canal into

Mansilla de las Mulas (**36.5km**, 801m) (accommodation, albergue, refreshments, camping, cycle shop, station).

> The 'new' town of **Mansilla de las Mulas** (pop 1800) was established in 1181 beside a crossing point of the río Esla as part of the repopulation of northern Spain following the Christian Reconquest. The town was surrounded by great walls up to 14m high and 3m thick with six defensive towers and four

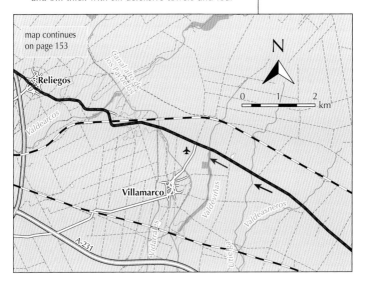

map continues on page 153

protected gateways, one of which opened directly onto the medieval bridge over the Esla. Large parts of the walls together with some of the towers and two gateways are still extant. The town celebrates several annual festivals, including the 'tomato' fair on the last Sunday in August. In the morning, there is an agricultural show together with prizes for the best tomatoes while in the afternoon the youth of the town participate in tomato warfare in the meadows by the river.

Go ahead over crossroads past pilgrim monument L and through gap in city walls into pedestrian zone. Turn first R and immediately L (Calle de Santa Maria) passing church R. Emerge into Plaza del Pozo and continue ahead (Calle del Puente). At end continue onto main road (N-601) and leave town across bridge over río Esla. Join senda L and continue past roundabout to beginning of **Villamoros de Mansilla** (**41km**, 801m), where senda ends, and cycle on road through village. Rejoin senda beyond village and after 400 metres, follow this forking L beside restaurant (accommodation, refreshments) to

The mighty walls surrounding medieval Mansilla de las Mulas

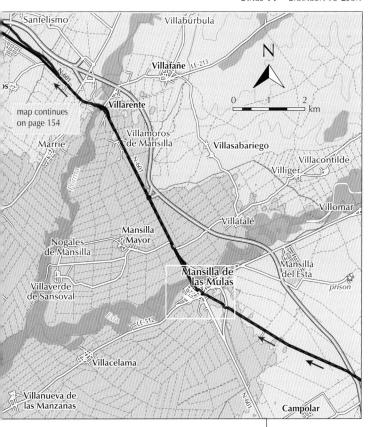

map continues
on page 154

cross pedestrian bridge over río Porma. After bridge turn
R under main road and L to cycle along R of road and
continue through **Villarente** (**42.5km**, 801m) (accommodation, albergue, refreshments) eventually joining service
road R.

Just before end of service road, bear R on gravel track
and follow this through scrubland. Go ahead over crossroads then pass under motorway and ascend steeply into
Arcahueja (**46.5km**, 843m) (accommodation, albergue,

153

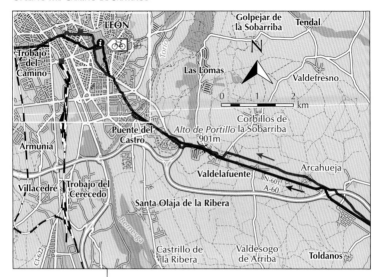

refreshments). Continue ascending past **Valdelafuente** L (**48km**, 867m) (refreshments) then turn L at crossroads and pass between industrial units to reach N-601 main road. Turn R and bear R on track beside road and ascend past roundabout L to reach **Alto de Portillo summit** (901m) overlooking León. Follow track turning L on footbridge over main road and continue on other side. Bear R, passing roundabout R and follow track beside road over motorway. At next roundabout, turn L and R over first exit then continue ahead beside main road. Where track ends, join main road (Ave Madrid), following this into **Puente del Castro** (**52.5km**, 815m) (albergue, refreshments).

Opposite San Pedro church R, fork L (Calle Victoriano Martínez) to reach T-junction. Go ahead over crossroads and cross río Torio by pedestrian bridge. Turn R at T-junction and L to regain main road (now Ave Alcalde Miguel Castaño) into suburbs of León. Continue ahead over first roundabout, then at second roundabout (with Santa Anna fountain in middle) bear L ahead (Calle Rollo Santa Anna, fourth exit, sp centro urbano). Pass small

Parque Santa Anna R and fork R (Calle Barahona, one-way street). ▶ Go ahead over crossroads through line of city walls and continue ahead (Calle Puerta Moneda, becoming Calle la Rúa). Emerge into Plaza San Marcelo, with Gaudí designed Casa Botines ahead, and turn R (Calle Ancha) beside Guzmanes palace to reach Plaza de Regla in front of cathedral in **León** (**55km**, 840m) (accommodation, albergue, youth hostel, refreshments, camping, tourist office, cycle shop, station).

The route described here goes the 'wrong way' along a series of one-way streets: walk your cycle or use the road route described below to reach the cathedral.

LEÓN

San Isidoro basilica houses the mausoleum of the kings of León

During the Roman occupation, León (pop 126,000) was the military capital of Spain and home city of the VII legion for almost 350 years. After the Romans left (AD476) the city went into decline and was captured by the Moors in AD712. Although reconquered in AD754, its position near the fighting line meant it was not repopulated until AD856. By the beginning of the 10th century the kingdom of León was dominant in north-west Spain and a golden era had begun, enhanced by union with Castile in 1230. Two of the city's four iconic buildings – Santa María cathedral and San Isidoro basilica – date from this period. The cathedral, which was based on Reims cathedral and is the leading example of French Gothic style in Spain, was built between 1205–1301. Inside it has one of the greatest collections of medieval stained glass in the world. San Isidoro basilica, in Romanesque style, which houses the mausoleum of the kings of León, has been described as 'the Sistine chapel of Romanesque style'.

San Marcos monastery, begun in 1515 as headquarters of the military order of St James, has one of the finest Plateresque façades in Spain. Nowadays it houses a parador, one of a chain of state-owned hotels inside historic buildings. Gaudí's Casa Botines represents León's more recent period of prosperity fuelled by the exploitation of coal in the nearby mountains during the late 19th century. Built in 1891 in neo-Gothic/modernist style as both a residence and a commercial warehouse, it is situated both literally and metaphorically between the old town and the late 19th-century extension. It is one of only three Gaudí buildings outside of Catalonia, but do not worry if you miss it, there is another even better example: the Episcopal palace in Astorga at the end of the next stage!

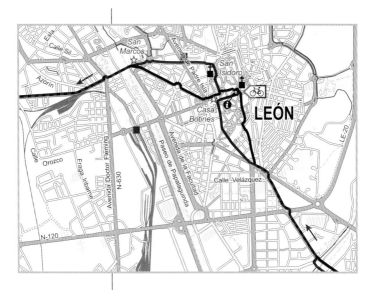

Road route

From Trinidad church in **Sahagún**, cycle E and turn L (Calle la Herrería) to reach crossroads. Turn R and fork immediately L (Calle Antonio Nicolás). Pass Santa Cruz monastery R and continue past Arco de San Benito gateway (visible 100 metres R along first side street), out of town. Bear R over río Cea on Puente Canto bridge and continue ahead past campsite R. Bear R at roundabout (N-120, sp León), then pass under road bridge and turn L (second exit, N-120, sp León) at next roundabout to

reach N-120 main road. Continue for 2km to pass side road that leads across motorway to **Calzada del Coto** (1km away R). Cross line of Camino then turn sharply R on side road and after 100 metres L onto Camino on tree-lined gravel senda L. Continue ahead parallel with motorway R, following this under high-speed railway line. Continue over irrigation canal gently uphill to reach **Bercianos del Real Camino** (**10.5km**, 857m) (albergue, refreshments).

Fork R at beginning of village, passing between built-up area L and fire brigade tower R. At end of village,

Canal Bajo de los Payuelos irrigation canal

rejoin road with parallel tree-lined senda and follow this ahead ascending gently through fields. Pass under motorway and railway to reach edge of **El Burgo Ranero** (**17.5km**, 880m) (accommodation, albergue, refreshments, station).

Dogleg R and L to follow Calle Real through centre of village. After village, rejoin shaded track and follow this through fields. Pass turn-off for Villamarco (**25.5km**, 864m), then cross Canal alto de los Payuelos irrigation canal and pass under railway. Continue winding through fields, descending gently to **Reliegos** (**30.5km**, 825m) (albergue, refreshments). Fork L (Calle Real) through village then continue on track crossing motorway. At end of shaded track, fork L to cross bridge over Mansilla de las Mulas bypass. Follow road over irrigation canal into **Mansilla de las Mulas** (**36.5km**, 801m) (accommodation, albergue, refreshments, camping, cycle shop, station).

Turn L at T-junction and R onto main road (N-601, sp León), passing through town. Continue through gate in city walls and across bridge over río Esla. Go ahead to T-junction and turn L on N-601.3 ◀ Go ahead over roundabout and continue through **Villamoros de Mansilla** (**41km**, 801m) and **Villarente** (**42.5km**, 801m) (accommodation, albergue, refreshments), using service road R. Ascend steadily, passing under A-60 motorway and continue through **Arcahueja** (**46.5km**, 843m) (accommodation, albergue, refreshments) and **Valdelafuente** L (**48km**, 867m) (refreshments). Go ahead over roundabout, where road becomes dual carriageway, to reach **Alto de Portillo summit** (901m). Start descending, with views of León ahead then follow main road ahead over roundabout (second exit). Cross motorway bridge and go ahead again at next roundabout (second exit) into Ave Madrid descending through **Puente del Castro** (**52.5km**, 815m) (albergue, refreshments).

Cross long bridge over río Torio and continue on Ave Alcalde Miguel Castaño into suburbs of León. Continue ahead over first roundabout, then at second roundabout (with Santa Anna fountain in middle) bear L ahead (Calle Rollo Santa Anna, fourth exit, sp centro urbano). ◀ Just

The N-601 is a busy main road with a wide hard shoulder providing a good cycle lane.

The route avoiding one-way streets starts here.

before Parque Santa Anna R, turn R into pedestrianised Calle Santa Anna. Pass yellow Santa Anna church L and fork R on one-way system. Cycle through Plaza del Riaño, passing through bollards uphill on cobbles, then turn R (Calle de la Santa Cruz) and follow this bearing L into Plaza Mayor. Continue ahead along L side of square into Calle Mariano Domínguez Berrueta and pass seminary and Episcopal's palace R to reach Plaza de Regla in front of cathedral in **León** (**54.5km**, 840m) (accommodation, albergue, youth hostel, refreshments, tourist office, cycle shop, station).

León cathedral is the leading example of French Gothic style in Spain

159

STAGE 12
León to Astorga

Start	León cathedral (840m)
Finish	Astorga cathedral (870m)
Distance	47.5km; road route 48km
Ascent	346m; road route 325m
Descent	316m; road route 295m

Although still on the meseta, this is a greener stage that, after leaving the suburbs of León, climbs over a low agricultural plateau before descending gently into the well-irrigated Páramo basin. The route then undulates over two more ridges before descending to Astorga. Sendas beside the N-120 road are followed throughout while the road route uses the N-120 itself.

Camino route

From Plaza del Regala outside W face of cathedral in **León**, head W on pedestrianised Calle Sierra-Pambley and fork immediately R (Calle Dámaso Merino). Dogleg R and L into Calle Ordoño IV el Malo and at end turn R (Calle Cid). Bear R across Plaza San Isidoro into cobbled Calle del Sacramento, passing basilica of San Isidoro L. Bear L (Calle Abadía) and continue over traffic lights into Calle Renueva. ◀ Go ahead at crossroads (Ave Suero de Quiñones) to reach major roundabout.

Calle Renueva is a one-way street; walk your cycle on the pavement.

Pass L of roundabout then cross road and follow track into gardens opposite (Plaza de San Marcos). ◀ Pass monastery of San Marcos (now a luxury hotel) R and continue over río Bernesga on Puente de San Marcos bridge. Pass Parque de Quevedo R, then go ahead at roundabout into Ave Párroco Pablo Diez. Just before second roundabout, cross road and join cycle track passing L of roundabout then continue on footbridge over railway. Rejoin main road (Calle Real) and follow this through León suburb of **Trobajo del Camino** (**4km**, 841m) (accommodation, refreshments, cycle shop).

The road route joins here.

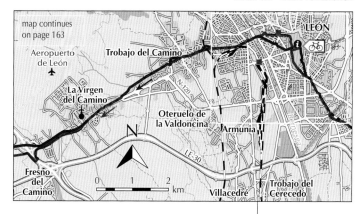

Turn L beside building 265 (Calle Colón) then immediately R (Plaza Sira San Pedro) and continue uphill.
Dogleg L and R across main road uphill (Camino la
Cruz). Pass between grass-covered old wine bodegas and
follow road past Leclerc hypermarket L to reach N-120
main road. Bear R onto service road then join main
road ascending into **La Virgen del Camino** (**7km**, 909m)
(accommodation, albergue, refreshments). Opposite
modern church R with tall concrete spire, fork L (Calle la
Paz), dropping down beside main road.

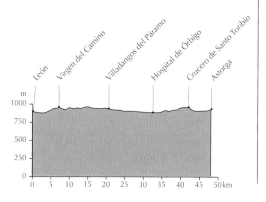

The 300m long medieval bridge in Hospital de Órbigo

Alternative route from La Virgen del Camino to Puente de Órbigo

From La Virgen del Camino, an alternative waymarked route (not shown on the map for this stage) that avoids walking beside the N-120 main road heads SW on tracks and quiet roads to Villar de Mazarife (14km, 869m) on the edge of the Páramo before descending to rejoin the main route at Puente de Órbigo (28km). This route is 3km longer than the main route.

Go ahead over two mini-roundabouts, then where road bears L into new development of Truevano, continue ahead on gravel road. Fork R, descending steeply to cross stream, then bear L through scrubland and pass under A-66 motorway. Turn R beside motorway R, then follow track winding through scrubland. Go ahead over cross-roads to reach main road and bear L on senda beside N-120 to reach **Valverde de la Virgen** (**11.5km**, 891m) (albergue, refreshments) where senda ends. ◄

The bell tower of the church on the right at the beginning of the village is covered with storks' nests.

Cycle uphill through village on main road, then fork L on gravel track slightly away from road. Zig-zag R and L to reach senda and continue to **San Miguel del Camino**

162

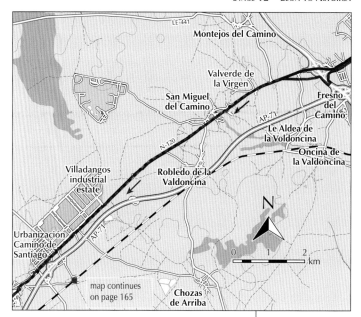

(**13km**, 899m) (refreshments). Again join road through village, regaining senda L after end of built-up area. Soon reach summit (922m) then pass modern industrial estate and **Urbanización Camino de Santiago** housing development (accommodation, refreshments) both R and follow asphalt service road to beginning of **Villadangos del Páramo** (**20.5km**, 899m) (accommodation, albergue, refreshments, camping, station).

Cross main road and fork R (Calle Real) through village. Cross bridge over canal del Páramo and follow gravel track ahead through trees, soon returning to main road. Cross road to follow senda L of road and continue to **San Martín del Camino** (**25km**, 869m) (albergue, refreshments). At end of village, turn R beside irrigation canal and immediately L on senda. Dogleg over small irrigation ditch then turn R beside derelict farm building back to main road. Continue on senda for 3.75km, then just before large Seat dealership L, follow track turning R through fields. Emerge on asphalt road then go ahead over crossroads onto cobbled road (Calle de Paso Honroso) across '**Roman bridge**' over río Órbigo, and continue into **Hospital de Órbigo** (**32km**, 821m) (accommodation, albergue, refreshments, camping).

> **Hospital de Órbigo** (pop 1000) is located where the old Roman road from León–Astorga (two important cities in Roman Spain) crossed the río Órbigo, which before the Barrios de Luna dam in the mountains upstream was commissioned in 1951 carried a much greater flow than it does nowadays. Although known as the 'Roman bridge', the current bridge with 19 arches is medieval, having being erected in the 13th century. The ruins of a pilgrim hospital founded by the order of San Juan of Jerusalem stand close to the bridge.

Cycle through village on Calle Álvarez Vega (cobbled), going ahead over two crossroads. Fork L then leave village on gravel track ahead through fields. Bear R and continue on senda beside main road. Pass road junction and join asphalt of old road beside main road. Briefly join main road, then return to old road. Where this ends,

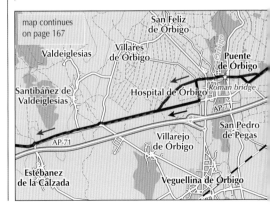

continue ahead on gravel track, then turn L across main road by orange bus shelter at roundabout and follow old road again, now on opposite side. Ascend over two ridges, then after 3km, turn back across main road and turn L across side road, regaining old road. Where this ends, bear R away from main road on gravel track through open woodland ascending to reach summit (916m) at **Crucero de Santo Toribio** R, with view of Astorga ahead. Descend steeply to road junction and continue on N-120a through

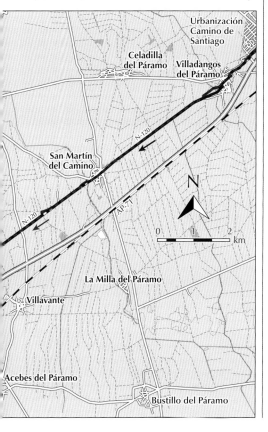

Crucero de Santo Toribio cross marks the spot where Bishop Toribio fell to his knees when banished from Astorga

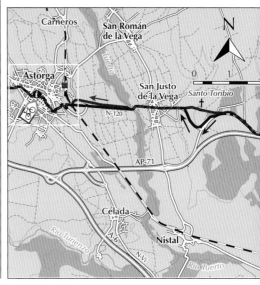

San Justo de la Vega (**43.5km**, 851m) (accommodation, refreshments).

After village, cross río Tuerto using pedestrian bridge beside road. After 150 metres, turn R then bear L and continue behind industrial units L. Cross stone bridge then bear L on asphalt road to reach T-junction beside railway line. ▶ Use zigzag ramps to cross railway and descend back to road. Turn L before second

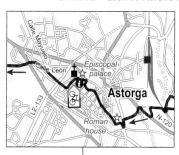

railway line, then turn R at T-junction and cross disused railway. Turn L at roundabout (Travesía de Minerva, third exit), then turn L (Calle Perpetua Socorro) at T-junction. After 80 metres, turn sharply R (Calle Puerta del Sol) steeply uphill into beginning of Astorga. Turn R (Calle de los Padres Redentoristas) past Santa Vera Cruz chapel R to reach Plaza Major. Cycle diagonally L across square to leave by narrow street on opposite corner. Go over cross-

There is a disused level crossing here which has been closed permanently since the line was upgraded to take high-speed trains.

roads, then fork L (Calle de Postas) and R (Calle de Santiago). Turn R at end in front of Colegio Santa Marta and L into Plaza Eduardo de Castro, passing Episcopal palace R to reach cathedral in **Astorga** (**47.5km**, 870m) (accommodation, albergue, refreshments, tourist office, cycle shop, station).

Road route

From Plaza del Regala outside W face of cathedral in **León**, head W on pedestrianised Calle Sierra Pambley and fork immediately R (Calle Dámaso Merino). Dogleg R and L into Calle Ordoño IV el Malo and at

ASTORGA

Ruins of Roman Astorga, a wealthy mining town

Astorga (pop 11,200), known to the Romans as Asturica Augusta, grew prosperous due to its position near to Roman gold mines. The city had paved streets, some covered with porticos, while a system of canals brought fresh water down from the mountains and underground sewers took the waste away. Part of the walls that surrounded the Roman city still stand and ongoing excavations are uncovering other Roman buildings and artefacts including baths, sewers and mosaic floors. All this ended with the collapse of the Roman Empire and similar levels of urban development did not reappear for over 1000 years.

The city went into a prolonged period of decline. Tribal overlords came and went and for 50 years the city was controlled by the Moors. After they were expelled, it was another 100 years before Christian repopulation began. A cathedral was built (Astorga had been a bishopric since Roman conversion to Christianity) and churches, convents and pilgrim hospitals were founded to care for the growing number of pilgrims on their way to Santiago. Astorga became an important stopover on the Camino as pilgrims spent several days preparing for the hard crossing of the Montes de León.

The cathedral of Santa María was started in 1069 with much later rebuilding and extension giving a mix of Gothic, Renaissance and Baroque styles. Across the road from the cathedral, the Episcopal palace is a relatively recent addition to the cityscape. After the old palace was destroyed by fire in 1886, Antoni Gaudí (an old friend of the bishop) was commissioned to design a replacement. Built in neo-Gothic/modernist style using grey granite, the building is a cross between a castle and a palace. As one of the architect's early commissions it is rather plain compared with some of his later works in Barcelona, but nevertheless it is a spectacular building. Despite it being intended as both administrative building for the diocese and home for the bishop, it was never used as a residence and nowadays holds a museum.

end turn L (Calle Cid) and immediately R (Calle de los Pilotos Regueral). Go ahead over crossroads, passing Gaudí-designed Casa Botines L to reach Plaza de Santo Domingo roundabout.

Take third exit (Gran Vía de San Marcos) then continue ahead over next roundabout (fourth exit). At end cross dual carriageway into Plaza de San Marcos and continue across square passing in front of monastery of San Marcos (now a luxury hotel) R. ▶ Continue over río Bernesga on Puente de San Marcos bridge. Pass Parque de Quevedo R, then go ahead at roundabout into Ave Párroco Pablo Diez. Just before second roundabout, join cycle track R and follow this crossing first exit and continuing over railway bridge into **Trobajo del Camino** (**4km, 841m**) (accommodation, refreshments, cycle shop).

The camino route is joined here.

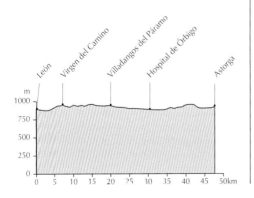

Where cycle track ends, turn R (Pl la Ermita) before small chapel. At end, turn L and R (Calle de la Fuente) then first L (Calle la Para). Go ahead over three cross-roads then turn L (Dr Vega Fernández) at fourth. At end turn R and follow main road bearing L, then turn R uphill (Camino la Cruz) beside house 358. Pass between grass-covered old wine bodegas and follow road past Leclerc hypermarket L to reach N-120 main road. Bear R onto service road then join main road ascending into **La Virgen del Camino** (**7km**, 909m) (accommodation, albergue, refreshments).

Pass modern concrete church with tall spire R then continue on road, using hard shoulder, to pass through complicated motorway junction following sp N-120 Astorga. ◄ Stay on main road through **Valverde de la Virgen** (**11km**, 891m) (albergue, refreshments) and **San Miguel del Camino** (**12km**, 899m) (refreshments).

Pass extensive factory developments R before reaching roundabout at beginning of **Urbanización Camino de Santiago** housing development (accommodation, refreshments). Join service road R of main road, passing through petrol station, then at next roundabout turn L across road to join service road on opposite side. Follow this to beginning of **Villadangos del Páramo** (**20km**, 899m) (accommodation, albergue, refreshments, camping).

Rejoin main road, then fork second R (Calle Real) through village. Turn third L (opposite house 44) into Travesía Calle Real, then R at end to rejoin main road. Continue to **San Martín del Camino** (**24km**, 869m) (albergue, refreshments). Cycle on main road for 6km, then turn R at crossroads (sp Puente de Órbigo). Bear L beside brick watertower then go ahead over crossroads onto cobbled road (Calle de Paso Honroso) across 'Roman bridge' over río Órbigo to reach **Hospital de Órbigo** (**31km**, 821m) (accommodation, albergue, refreshments, camping).

Cycle through village on Calle Álvarez Vega, then go ahead at crossroads and turn L (Calle Cortes de León) at T-junction. ◄ Continue to main road (N-120) and turn R. Start ascending and at first roundabout, bear R (sp Santibáñez de Valdeiglesias) onto old course of main

Cycles are allowed on the N-120, but not on any other part of the junction.

The camino route goes ahead here on a gravel track.

road. Ignore turn R, keeping ahead uphill beside N-120, then at second roundabout with orange bus shelter, cross N-120 to join old course, now L of road. Where road comes close to motorway at top of hill, rejoin N-120. Go ahead over side road then follow main road round sweeping bend L and fork R (sp Astorga centro urbano) continuing downhill with view of Astorga ahead. Pass through **San Justo de la Vega** (**43.5km**, 851m) (accommodation, refreshments).

After village, cross río Tuerto then go ahead over roundabout to reach railway line. ▶ Turn L up zigzag ramps to cross railway and descend back to road. Turn L before second railway line, then turn R at T-junction and cross disused railway. Turn L at roundabout (Travesía Minerva, third exit), then turn L (Calle Perpetua Socorro) at T-junction. After 80 metres, turn sharply R (Calle Puerta del Sol) steeply uphill into beginning of Astorga. Turn R (Calle de los Padres Redentoristas) past Santa Vera Cruz chapel R to reach Plaza Major. Cycle diagonally L across square to leave by narrow street on opposite corner. Go over crossroads, then fork L (Calle de Postas) and R (Calle de Santiago). Turn R at end in front of Colegio Santa Marta and L into Plaza Eduardo de Castro, passing Episcopal palace R, to reach cathedral in **Astorga** (**48km**, 870m) (accommodation, albergue, refreshments, tourist office, cycle shop, station).

There is a disused level crossing here which has been closed permanently since the line was upgraded to take high-speed trains.

The Episcopal palace was designed by Antoni Gaudí for his friend the Bishop of Astorga

STAGE 13
Astorga to Ponferrada

Start	Astorga cathedral (870m)
Finish	Ponferrada, town hall (544m)
Distance	54km; road route 54.5km
Ascent	824m; road route 801m
Descent	1150m; road route 1127m

This stage starts by using sendas to climb steadily onto the remote moorland of the Maragateria, part of the Montes de León, reaching the highest point of the Camino (1507m). This ascent is followed by a steep descent on a minor road into the Bierzo basin that provides an exhilarating ride with no need to pedal for 15km. A series of small villages are passed with many abandoned properties reflecting continuing population decline. The road route follows a quiet country road (LE-142) throughout.

Camino route
From W front of cathedral in **Astorga**, follow one-way street Calle de la Portería SW. Turn second R (Calle Puerta

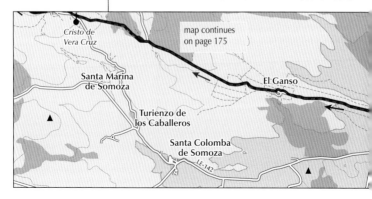

map continues
on page 175

Obispo) beside yellow ochre coloured Sancti Spiritus convent R. Continue over crossroads through Plaza Escritores Carro Celada into Calle San Pedro, then go ahead over main road (Calle de los Mártires, sp Castrillo) out of town. Pass **Valdeviejas** R and **ermita del Ecce Homo chapel** L then cross motorway and join senda R to reach village sign at beginning of **Murias de Rechivaldo** (**4km**, 884m) (accommodation, albergue, refreshments).

Fork L on gravel track, soon becoming brick block, through village. At village end pass through bollards onto gravel track and follow this through scrubland to crossroads. Go ahead (sp Santa Catalina) on gravel senda and continue to village sign for Santa Catalina. Fork R through bollards and follow gravel track, soon becoming brick-block road, through **Santa Catalina de Somoza** (**8.5km**, 983m) (albergue, refreshments).

At end of village, rejoin road and continue to reach village sign for El Ganso. Fork R on asphalt side road through **El Ganso** (**12.5km**, 1019m) (albergue, refreshments). Bear L in village passing church R, then turn R to rejoin road and continue on senda through open country. Fork L (sp Rabanal del Camino) then follow gravel track briefly away from road. ▶ Return to roadside and pass **Cristo de Vera Cruz chapel** L then fork R on concrete side road to pass through **Rabanal del Camino** (**19.5km**, 1158m) (accommodation, albergue, refreshments).

This track is known as Via Crucis and is lined with handmade crosses woven into the fence.

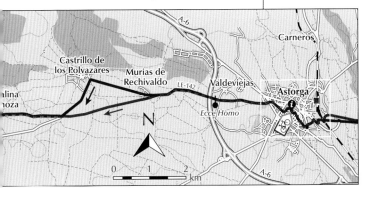

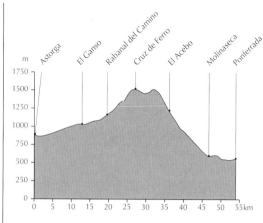

Foncebadon is a
semi-ghost village
where many
properties have
been abandoned.

At end of village pass old wash-house R, then continue on gravel track steeply uphill taking different route across scrubby hillside from that of main road. Cross and re-cross road, then after third crossing continue ahead through **Foncebadon** L (**25km**, 1420m) (albergue, refreshments). ◀ Continue ahead, crossing road again

There are long stretches of senda on the ascent into the Montes de León

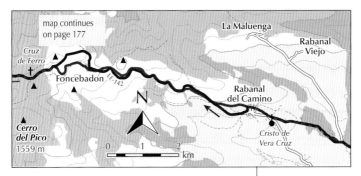

to reach huge pile of stones and **Cruz de Ferro** (**27km**, 1499m).

> **Cruz de Ferro** is an iron cross atop a tall mast rising from a great mound of stones. Tradition has it that pilgrims should bring a stone from home and then toss it over their shoulders onto the mound; this is said to signify freeing themselves from carrying the burden of sin. Although not the highest point (that is at an unmarked spot over 5km further on), the views are stunning.

Follow gravel senda gently across plateau passing through abandoned village of **Manjarin** (**29.5km**, 1441m) (albergue) and then climbing to pass below **Collado de las Antenas** hilltop covered in communications masts R to reach summit at **Peña de la Escurpia** (**31.5km**, 1507m) (pop-up café). ▶ Follow road as it descends steeply round a series of sweeping bends and pass through pretty village of **El Acebo** (**36.5km**, 1149m) (accommodation, albergue, refreshments). Further down, pass just above **Riego de Ambrós** (**40km**, 940m) (accommodation, albergue, refreshments) then negotiate a series of hairpins to reach beginning of **Molinaseca** (**46km**, 585m) (accommodation, albergue, refreshments, tourist office).

> The track beyond the summit descends very steeply and is not suitable for cyclists who should use the road to reach Molinaseca.

> **Molinaseca** (pop 900) stands in an attractive position beside the Puente de los Peregrinos old stone

175

bridge over the río Meruelo. Its position at the foot of the Montes de León made it an important pilgrim stopover to recover from the crossing (or to prepare themselves for the return journey on the way back from Santiago!) and it was well provided with churches and a pilgrim hospital.

Turn L off main road over old stone bridge and continue through centre of village on Calle Real. At end of village pass pilgrim monument R and bear L to regain main road. Continue downhill, then ascend over small rise. At summit, fork L downhill on gravel track, then ascend to **Campo** (**50km**, 550m).

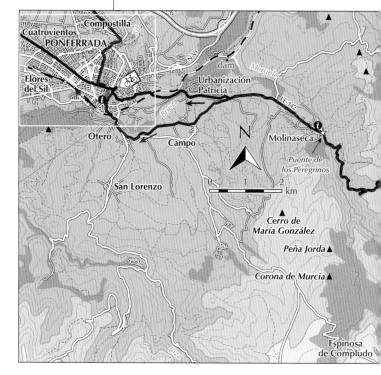

The 15km descent includes a series of hairpins

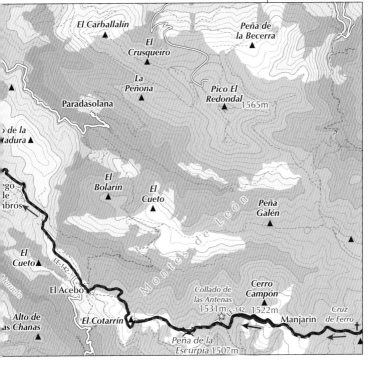

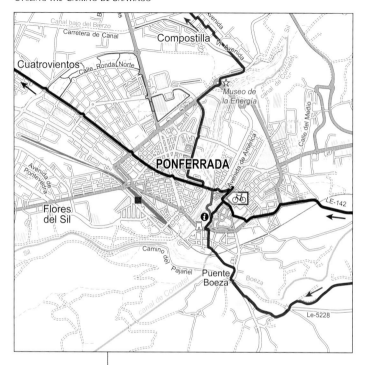

Fork L here (Calle Tras la Cava) to bypass town centre and connect directly with next stage at río Sil bridge.

Fork L and immediately R (Calle Real) and continue to Plaza la Plazolica. Dogleg L and R then follow asphalt road out of village. Continue to angled crossroads and bear R (Carretera los Barrios de Salas). At T-junction, bear R onto main road then go ahead over mini-roundabout and turn R across second bridge over río Boeza. Turn L beside river (Calle Camino bajo de San Andrés) and continue under railway. Cycle steeply uphill and turn R (Calle el Hospital). Turn L at main road and immediately R (Calle Gil y Carrasco) uphill beside castle L, then fork R. ◄ Continue through Plaza Virgen de la Encina into Calle del Reloj and continue to Plaza Ayuntamiento in **Ponferrada** (**54km**, 544m) (accommodation, albergue, refreshments, tourist office, cycle shop, station).

Ponferrada (pop 66,000) grew out of an order by the bishop of Astorga in 1082 for the construction of a stone pilgrim bridge over the río Sil. A century later, when the Knights Templar were given the task of protecting the Camino, they built a castle on a hill overlooking the confluence of the río Boeza with the Sil. This still stands and is the dominant feature of the town. A small village developed around the bridge and castle, but it remained insignificant until the mid 20th century. Modern-day Ponferrada is an industrial city that grew rapidly between 1940 and 1970 as a result of Spanish government policy. Local coal was used to fuel two power stations and a steelworks, while other factories were established producing cement, glass and roofing slates. More recently, a large factory opened producing turbine blades for wind turbines.

Ponferrada castle was built by the Knights Templar

Road route

From W front of cathedral in **Astorga**, follow one-way street Calle de la Portería SW. Turn second R (Calle Puerta Obispo) beside yellow-ochre coloured Sancti

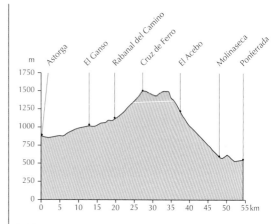

Spiritus convent R. Continue over crossroads through Plaza Escritores Carro Celada into Calle San Pedro, then go ahead over main road (Calle de los Mártires, sp Castrillo) out of town. Pass **Valdeviejas** R and **ermita del Ecce Homo chapel** L then cross motorway and continue through **Murias de Rechivaldo** (**4km**, 884m) (accommodation, albergue, refreshments).

Before entering **Castrillo de los Polvazares** (accommodation, albergue, refreshments) follow road bearing L (sp Santa Colomba de Somoza) and continue through scrubland to second crossroads. Turn R (sp Santa Catalina) on asphalt road with camino route on gravel senda R and continue to village sign for Santa Catalina. Bear L, following road through edge of **Santa Catalina de Somoza** (**9km**, 983m) (albergue, refreshments).

After village, road and camino routes come together again and continue to reach village sign for El Ganso. Fork R on asphalt side road through **El Ganso** (**13km**, 1019m) (albergue, refreshments). Bear L in village passing church R, then turn R to rejoin road and continue through open country. Fork L (sp Rabanal del Camino) then pass **Cristo de Vera Cruz chapel** L and fork R on concrete side road to pass through **Rabanal del Camino** (**20km**, 1158m) (accommodation, albergue refreshments).

Pass church L, then after 100 metres turn L down-hill on asphalt side road. After 100 metres turn R at T-junction then turn R onto main road. Continue uphill, now ascending more steeply and winding across hill-side. Cross and re-cross gravel camino route to reach third crossing. ▶ Continue ahead on road, passing **Foncebadon** L (**26km**, 1420m) (albergue, refreshments). On reaching summit plateau, road levels off. Continue past huge pile of stones and **Cruz de Ferro** R (**28km**, 1499m).

Follow road undulating gently across plateau pass-ing through abandoned village of **Manjarin** (**30.5km**, 1441m) (albergue) and then climb to pass below **Collado de las Antenas** hilltop covered in communications masts R to reach road summit at **Peña de la Escurpia** (**32.5km**, 1507m) (pop-up café). Follow road as it descends steeply round a series of sweeping bends and pass through pretty village of **El Acebo** (**38km**, 1149m) (accommodation, albergue, refreshments). Further down, pass just above **Riego de Ambrós** (**41.5km**, 940m) (accommodation, albergue, refreshments) then negotiate a series of hair-pins to reach beginning of **Molinaseca** (**47.5km**, 585m) (accommodation, albergue, refreshments, tourist office).

Turn L off main road over old stone bridge and con-tinue through centre of village on Calle Real. At end of vil-lage pass pilgrim monument R and bear L to regain main road. Continue downhill, then ascend over small rise and follow main road downhill past **Urbanización Patricia** housing development R. Cross río Boeza, then pass under railway bridge to reach roundabout at beginning of Ponferrada. Turn L (second exit) then go ahead over next roundabout (second exit). Turn first R (Calle Esteban de la Puente) then cross canal and turn R at T-junction (Calle de los Jardines) to reach Plaza Ayuntamiento in **Ponferrada** (**54.5km**, 544m) (accommodation, albergue, refreshments, tourist office, cycle shop, station).

To pass through the semi-ghost village of Foncebadon, where many properties have been abandoned, fork left here onto camino route and rejoin the road further on.

STAGE 14
Ponferrada to O Cebreiro

Start	Ponferrada, town hall (544m)
Finish	O Cebreiro church (1305m)
Distance	53km; road route 54.5km
Ascent	1046m; road route 988m
Descent	285m; road route 227m

This stage has two distinct sections. Leaving the industrial suburbs of Ponferrada, the Camino crosses the fertile El Bierzo basin, going through vineyards and past bodegas to reach Villafranca del Bierzo. Here it all changes as the route enters the steep-sided Valcarce valley, climbing gently at first but becoming increasingly steep, passing through small mountain communities to the mountain top hamlet of O Cebreiro on the border with Galicia. The road route follows the LE-713 out of Ponferrada and the N-VI road climbing the Valcarce valley.

Camino route

From W corner of Plaza del Ayuntamiento in **Ponferrada**, follow Calle Santa Beatriz de Silva N, soon bearing R downhill. At bottom of hill, turn sharply L (Calle General Vives) continuing downhill. Go ahead over roundabout (second exit) and cross bridge over río Sil. On opposite bank, turn first R downhill (Calle río Urdiales) then bear L passing carpark R. Turn R onto dual carriageway Ave Huertas then go ahead (second exit) at first roundabout and turn R (first exit) at second roundabout with stele in middle. Go ahead again at third roundabout, passing Museo de la Energía in old power station R. Turn L at mini-roundabout and after 250 metres, fork R into **Compostilla** (**3km**, 539m). ◄

Compostilla is a garden village with houses, church and sports facilities built originally for employees at a nearby factory.

Turn R at end and immediately L, on path passing through archway under house. At end turn L past church

182

An old power station in Ponferrada is now a museum dedicated to energy

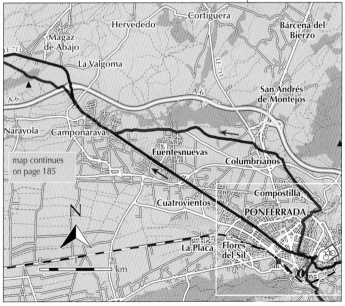

map continues
on page 185

183

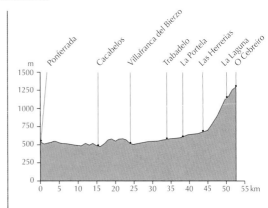

and R on track beside church R. Go ahead over next road then turn L at end. Turn immediately R beside sports club and continue ahead over crossroads onto track. Emerge on road and bear R. Fork R at junction of tracks then continue behind large hotel R and under road bridge (accommodation, refreshments). Follow asphalt surface, forking L at next track junction, continuing through vineyards. Pass church L then, where road turns L, go ahead to cross dual carriageway main road and continue (Calle de la Iglesia) into **Columbrianos** (**5km**, 526m) (albergue, refreshments).

Bear R at road junction, then after 100 metres, fork L (Calle San Blas) beside ermita de San Blas y San Roque chapel out of village, continuing through smallholdings and vineyards to reach **Fuentesnuevas** (**7.5km**, 508m) (refreshments). Pass small chapel L, then follow Calle Real ahead through edge of village and continue through smallholdings to reach main road. Bear R (Ave Camino de Santiago) through **Camponaraya** (**10km**, 493m) (albergue, refreshments).

Go ahead over two roundabouts and immediately after second, fork L beside wine bodega L on asphalt track between shade trees. Cross motorway and follow gravel track ahead winding through vineyards (pop-up café). Go ahead over crossroads and continue ahead on road into **Cacabelos** (**15.5km**, 485m) (accommodation,

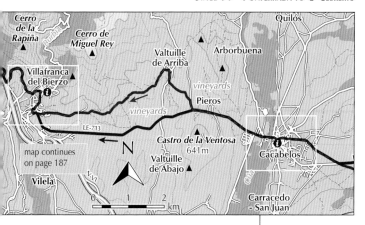

albergue, refreshments, tourist office, cycle shop).

> **Cacabelos** (pop 5300) lies in the middle of the small wine-producing region of El Bierzo. Grapes were introduced to the area by the Romans and developed during the Middle Ages by monasteries, particularly those of the Cistercian order. After late 19th-century devastation by phylloxera, new vines were planted and the region now produces mostly soft red wines from local mencía grapes and white from doña blanca and godello varieties.

Cycle through town on Calle Cimadevilla, becoming Calle Santa María where it enters narrow streets of old town. Pass church R and fork R (Calle de las Angustias), then emerge on main road and continue ahead over río Cúa, out of town. Road ascends steadily through vineyards past **Pieros** (**17.5km**, 541m) (albergue, refreshments). At top of hill, fork R (sp Valtuille de Arriba) and after 250 metres fork L on rocky track through

vineyards. Emerge on asphalt road and bear R into **Valtuille de Arriba** (**19.5km**, 557m) (accommodation, refreshments).

Fork L in village (Calle la Platería) and L again (Calle Camino de Santiago). Cross bridge over river then turn L and continue out of village on stony track that undulates steeply over three vineyard covered ridges. Emerge on road and follow this downhill to edge of Villafranca. Pass Santiago church L, descending on cobbled Calle Santiago to reach main road opposite castle. Bear R and follow Calle del Castillo winding downhill past castle L to mini-roundabout. Bear R and follow road ahead winding through narrow streets to reach Plaza Mayor in **Villafranca del Bierzo** (**24km**, 511m) (accommodation, albergue, refreshments, camping, tourist office, cycle shop).

VILLAFRANCA DEL BIERZO

Villafranca del Bierzo (pop 3100), literally 'town of the Franks in Bierzo', gets its name from the large number of French monks and pilgrims who visited the Bierzo between the 11th and 13th centuries when the abbey of Cluny was the main promoter of the pilgrimage. Finding the area to have the most agreeable climate of the whole Camino (not as hot and dry as the meseta, not as wet as Galicia), many of them stayed permanently. They built churches, monasteries and pilgrim hospitals and brought with them experience in wine making. The Church of Santiago has a Puerta del Perdón (Door of Forgiveness) where pilgrims who had become too ill to complete the journey to Santiago could gain absolution. It still opens, but nowadays only in jubilee years (years when St James's day falls on a Sunday). The castle is a later addition to the town, having being built in the early 16th century to replace a previous castle on the same site. Although it looks like a military structure, its principal function has always been as a residence for the Marqués de Villafranca.

Continue ahead (Calle San Nicolás) past large San Nicolás church and gardens (both R), then follow road bending L past Santa María church L. Go ahead onto via-duct and follow this turning R over río Burbia. Continue past Convento de la Concepción convent L and fork R (Calle Espiritu Santo). ▶ Follow road round wide bend of river to emerge beside A-6 motorway. Cross N-VI main road and follow cycle track behind concrete barriers L of road, gently climbing and winding beside motorway and river. ▶ Where barriers end, fork R off main road and, after 350 metres, fork R again to cycle through **Pereje** (**29.5km**, 550m) (albergue, refreshments), then rejoin main road. Where barriers end again (3km from Pereje) turn R across N-VI onto old course of road ascending through **Trabadelo** (**34km**, 574m) (albergue, refreshments).

You are now in the valley of the río Valcarce, which you will follow for the rest of the stage.

The N-VI was the old trunk road from Madrid to Coruña now almost devoid of traffic since the parallel A-6 motorway opened.

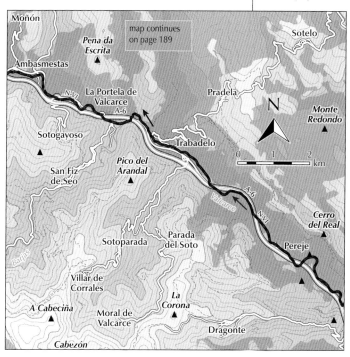

The Camino leaves Villafranca over the Puente Burbia

Continue on old road for 2.5km, then just before motorway viaduct, fork L down gravel bank and turn R to rejoin N-VI. Pass large Valcarce hotel and restaurant complex R and soon fork L to follow old road through **La Portela del Valcarce** (**38km**, 601m) (accommodation, albergue, refreshments). Rejoin main road after village, pass under motorway slip road and soon fork L back onto old road through **Ambasmestas** (**39km**, 615m) (accommodation, albergue, refreshments) and **Vega del Valcarce** (**40.5km**, 638m) (accommodation, albergue, refreshments). Rejoin main road (now numbered N-006A) and continue through **Ruitelán** (**43km**, 663m) (albergue, refreshments) to reach beginning of **Las Herrerías** (**44km**, 673m) (accommodation, albergue, refreshments).

Turn L downhill (sp La Faba) on quiet road. Follow road through **Hospital** (**45km**, 689m) (refreshments). At end of village keep ahead (sp La Faba) then bear L and start ascending very steeply on winding road. Pass turn-off L

The walking track is not suitable for cycles and should not be attempted.

where walking track heads uphill to La Faba. ◄ Continue uphill then turn sharply R (sp La Laguna) at road junction. Follow road round hairpin L, continuing steeply uphill round another hairpin to **La Laguna** (**51km**, 1149m)

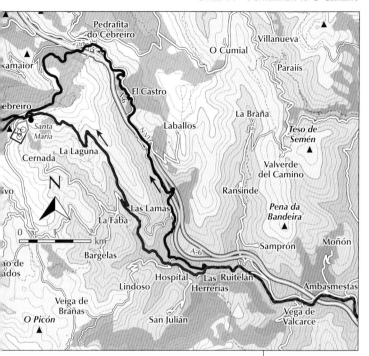

(albergue, refreshments). Follow road turning sharply R in village, continuing uphill on road along open hillside with views down Valcarce L. Emerge on summit plateau (1311m), then bear L on wider road and turn R into **O Cebreiro** (**53km**, 1305m) (accommodation, albergue, refreshments).

O CEBREIRO

The remote mountain top settlement of O Cebreiro played an important part in the 20th-century rediscovery of the Camino. The parish priest, Dr Elías Valiña Sampedro (1929–89) who was also an academic at the university of Salamanca, wrote his thesis on the Camino and became an expert

A reconstruction of an Iron Age palloza round house in O Cebreiro

in Compostelan studies. In 1971 he wrote his first guide for pilgrims and in 1984 started marking the entire route with the yellow arrows that have become synonymous with the Camino. After his death he was buried beside the church in O Cebreiro.

O Cebreiro attracts tourists to visit its reconstructed *pallozas* (pre-Roman Iron Age round houses) and to see the views over Galicia and the Bierzo. In common with many places on the Camino, the 11th-century church was built in Romanesque style by Clunaic monks from France.

Road route

From W corner of Plaza del Ayuntamiento in **Ponferrada**, follow Calle Santa Beatriz de Silva N, soon bearing R downhill. At bottom of hill, turn sharply L (Calle General Vives) continuing downhill. Go ahead over roundabout (second exit) and cross bridge over río Sil. Continue ahead (Ave de la Puebla) and go ahead over roundabout (Calle Camino de Santiago), then continue over mini-roundabout. At third roundabout continue ahead (LE713, Ave de Galicia) through **Cuatrovientos** (**3km**, 521m) and **Fuentesnuevas** (**5km**, 507m) to reach **Camponaraya** (**7.5km**, 493m) (albergue, refreshments).

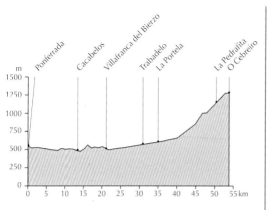

Go ahead over two roundabouts and follow main road bearing R out of town. Go ahead over two more roundabouts (part of motorway junction) and continue through **Magaz de Abajo** (**10km**, 501m). Immediately after 7km marker, fork R and follow road into **Cacabelos** (**13.5km**, 485m) (accommodation, albergue, refreshments, tourist office, cycle shop).

Cycle through town on Calle Cimadevilla, becoming Calle Santa María where it enters narrow streets of old town. Pass church R and fork R (Calle de las Angustias), then emerge on main road and continue ahead over río Cúa, out of town. Road ascends steadily through vineyards past **Pieros** (**15.5km**, 541m) (albergue, refreshments). Pass large bodega 'Adriá' L and after 400 metres, fork R (LE-713, sp Villafranca del Bierzo). Continue into town following Calle del Castillo winding downhill past castle L to mini-roundabout. Bear R and follow road ahead winding through narrow streets to reach Plaza Mayor in **Villafranca del Bierzo** (**21.5km**, 511m) (accommodation, albergue, refreshments, camping, tourist office, cycle shop).

Continue ahead (Calle San Nicolás) past large San Nicolás church and gardens (both R), then follow road bending L past Santa María church L. Go ahead onto viaduct and follow this turning R over río Burbia. Continue

The route passes through the vineyards of the Bierzo

past Convento de la Concepción L and fork R (Calle Espiritu Santo). Follow road round wide bend of river to emerge beside A-6 motorway and turn R along N-VI main road, gently climbing and winding beside motorway and river. After 2.5km fork R off main road and after 350 metres, fork R again to cycle through **Pereje** (**27km**, 550m) (albergue, refreshments), then rejoin main road. Continue for 3km then turn R onto old course of road ascending through **Trabadelo** (**31km**, 574m) (albergue, refreshments).

Continue on old road for 2.5km, then just before motorway viaduct, fork L down gravel bank and turn R to rejoin N-VI. Pass large Valcarce hotel and restaurant complex R and soon fork L to follow old road through **La Portela del Valcarce** (**35km**, 601m) (accommodation, albergue, refreshments). Rejoin main road after village, pass under motorway slip road and soon fork L back onto old road through **Ambasmestas** (**36.5km**, 615m) (accommodation, albergue, refreshments) and **Vega del Valcarce** (**38km**, 638m) (accommodation, albergue, refreshments). Rejoin main road (now numbered N-006A) and continue through **Ruitelán** (**40km**, 663m) (albergue, refreshments).

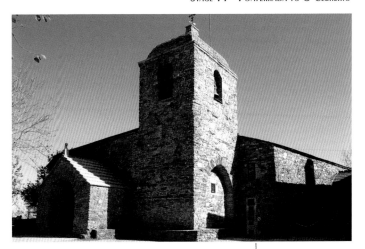

After 1km, where camino route forks L downhill, continue ahead winding uphill on N-006A. Pass through hamlet of **Las Lamas** (**43.5km**, 796m) and continue on road for 2km, passing under motorway twice. Fork L onto old route of N-VI continuing steeply uphill beside motorway, zigzagging through **El Castro** (**48km**, 1006m).

Continue uphill to reach roundabout at motorway junction. Go ahead (second exit, sp Pedrafita) past motorway service area L at **Pedrafita do Cebreiro** (**50.5km**, 1113m) (accommodation, refreshments).

Turn L at second roundabout (LU-633, second exit, sp Samos) on main road climbing steeply through forest. Once on summit plateau, fork L opposite bus layby onto side road, then follow this road bearing R into mountain top hamlet of **O Cebreiro** (**54.5km**, 1305m) (accommodation, albergue, refreshments).

O Cebreiro church was built in Romanesque style by monks from Cluny

STAGE 15
O Cebreiro to Sarria

Start	O Cebreiro church (1305m)
Finish	Sarria, Escalinata Maior steps (437m)
Distance	38km; road route 44.5km
Ascent	611m; road route 373m
Descent	1479m; road route 1241m

After crossing the high plateau of the Galician mountains, this stage descends via Triacastela into the Sarria valley, from where there are two options. Originally most pilgrims travelled via Samos with its great Benedictine monastery. The steady improvement of a shorter route via San Xil now attracts the majority of pilgrims. This guide offers both alternatives, with the camino route describing the route via San Xil using a mix of country lanes and woodland paths, while the road route follows the LU-633 (a quiet main road) via Samos. Both routes undulate throughout, although the prevailing grade is downhill.

Camino route
From church at **O Cebreiro**, follow cobbled track W through village and fork L passing above albergue R and through scrubland. Ascend steeply through woods and bear L at junction of tracks. Turn R at T-junction and follow asphalt road zigzagging down hillside to **Linares** (**3km**, 1221m) (albergue, refreshments). Join main road, then fork R at end of hamlet and after 100 metres turn L uphill onto track parallel with main road L. Follow this winding along below road, briefly running beside road past pilgrim monument L at **Alto do San Roque** (1270m), then climbing above road. Bear R to pass through **Hospital** (**5.5km**, 1242m) (albergue, refreshments).

Fork R in village, then pass church L and return to main road. Follow senda R of road for 1km, then fork

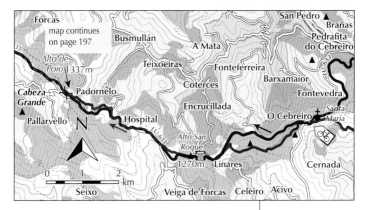

R downhill on side road. After 250 metres, turn L on track and follow this through woods. Bear R on road and where this ends at farm, continue on gravel track. Bear R on road through **Padornelo** (**8km**,1286m). Fork L in hamlet, ascending very steeply on gravel track to reach summit of main road at **Alto de Poio** (**8.5km**, 1337m) (accommodation, albergue, refreshments).

Continue on senda, eventually bearing R away from road through **Fonfría** (**12km**, 1292m) (albergue, refreshments). After village, follow track above main road through fields. Briefly emerge beside main road

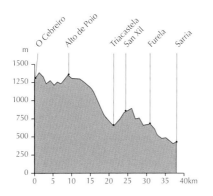

195

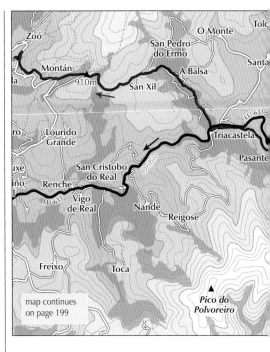

then follow track downhill and cross side road. Continue into **O Biduedo** (**14km**, 1185m) (albergue, refreshments).

Fork L at beginning of village then turn L at end of village to follow track winding steeply downhill through woods and fields for 2.5km. ◄ Continue into tiny hamlet of **Fillobal** (**17km**, 965m) (albergue, refreshments).

Turn sharply L in hamlet, continuing to reach side road. Bear L and after 30 metres, turn sharply R onto track through trees. Follow this parallel with but above main road, eventually dropping down L to cross road and continue into **Pasantes** (**18.5km**, 812m). Turn R at T-junction then fork L just before end of village. Follow winding tree-lined track downhill and fork R through Ramil. Bear L onto concrete road into **Triacastela** (**21km**, 663m) (accommodation, albergue, refreshments).

On the right below are the Triacastela quarries where limestone for Santiago's great buildings was obtained.

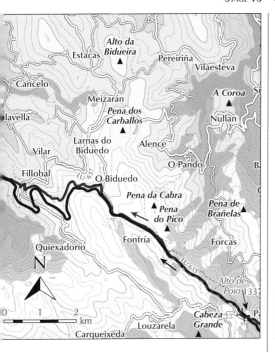

Quarries near Triacastela provided limestone for Santiago cathedral

197

At end of village, turn R at T-junction downhill to main road. Turn R and immediately L (sp San Xil) ascending past industrial area L to reach road junction. Fork R downhill then fork L on gravel track to reach El Beso hamlet (albergue). Continue past unusual square chapel L to **A Balsa** (**23km**, 734m) (albergue) and fork L on gravel track. Cross stream and turn R on concrete track through farmyard, then follow rocky track steeply uphill. Emerge on road and turn R, then L at T-junction and climb steeply through **San Xil** (**24.5km**, 860m).

The road to the left takes an easier route, winding down round a hairpin bend. Both routes join below the woods.

Follow road winding across plateau for 1.5km. Pass turn into forest R marked with yellow arrow then after 50 metres, where road bears L downhill, continue ahead on gravel track descending steeply through forest. ◄ Emerge on road beside small church R and turn R. After 100 metres, fork R on concrete track through **Montán** (**27.5km**, 754m) (albergue, refreshments).

Fork R then leave village on narrow lane between two stone barns following gravel track steeply downhill. Emerge on road and turn R. After 100 metres turn sharply L downhill on gravel sunken track between high banks. At bottom turn R at T-junction of tracks then cross **ford** with narrow stone causeway just wide enough to wheel cycle. Continue to road and bear L to reach **Furela** (**30.5km**, 664m) (refreshments).

Fork L through village on crazy paving stone track, then where this ends cross road and bear R on gravel track. At end of village rejoin road and bear L with Camino senda R of road. After 400 metres follow gravel track bearing R away from road, becoming rough concrete and descending through **Pintín** (**31.5km**, 630m) (accommodation, refreshments). Leave village on road downhill and just before this joins main road (which has bypassed village), fork R on gravel track. Continue downhill on sunken lane to arms of hairpin bend with church 100 metres L. Turn R and follow road down through woods around sharp bend L. ◄ Bear L using senda to pass roundabout R and continue downhill (sp Sarria). Fork R (sp Aguiada) and descend through **Aguiada** (**33.5km**, 497m) (albergue, refreshments).

The walking route goes ahead over the road, descending steps to cut off the hairpin bend.

Emerge beside main road and bear R on senda. Pass **San Mamede** L (**35km**, 490m) (albergue) and continue downhill to reach beginning of Sarria. Turn R at crossroads onto LU-633 main road then first L (Rúa Mestre Saavedra). Bear L, then turn R to reach roundabout in Plaza de Galicia. Fork R (Rúa do Peregrino, first exit) through housing development to cross Puente Riviera bridge over río Sarria. Turn R at T-junction (Rúa Beningo Quiroga) and after 40 metres turn L (Rúa Arrabaldo) through bollards to reach end of stage at bottom of Escalinata Maior steps in **Sarria** (**38km**, 437m) (accommodation, albergue, refreshments, camping, tourist office, cycle shop, station).

SARRIA

Santa Mariña church in Sarria

Medieval Sarria (pop 13,500) developed as an important stopover on the Camino, with churches, inns and bridges all built to aid the passage of pilgrims, while monks from the 13th-century Magdalena monastery founded a pilgrim hospital. When the pilgrimage declined from the mid 16th century, Sarria went into a prolonged period of recession. The Magdalena order was taken over by the Augustinians in 1568 then suppressed altogether in 1837, while the population fell to 350 in the 18th century. The coming of the railway (1880) brought a revival in Sarria's fortunes, providing wider markets for the town's agricultural production.

The modern-day pilgrimage has benefitted Sarria more than any other town, with the exception of Santiago. Almost half of all walking pilgrims start their journey from here, taking advantage of a rule that to qualify for a Compostela they must have walked continuously for 100km. Sarria, 113km from Santiago, is the first town with rail and bus services that lies outside this limit. As a result, there are a large number of albergues and hostels, particularly at the top of the town steps where the walking route to Santiago officially starts. Nevertheless, it is often difficult to find a bed during the peak season.

Road route

From **O Cebreiro**, follow LU-633 main road W descending through **Linares** (**3km**, 1221m) (albergue). Ascend to **Alto San Roque** (1270m), passing huge pilgrim monument on windswept (and often misty) hilltop. Descend again, then ascend steeply and bear R to pass through **Hospital** R (**5.5km**, 1242m) (albergue, refreshments). Rejoin main road after village, then descend and ascend again to reach road summit at **Alto de Poio** (8.5km, 1337m) (accommodation, albergue, refreshments). Continue past **Fonfría** (**12km**, 1284m) (accommodation, albergue, refreshments), then descend round series of hairpins past **Fillobal** (**18.5km**, 936m) (albergue, refreshments) and **Pasantes** (**20.5km**, 804m) to **Triacastela** (**23km**, 671m) (accommodation, albergue, refreshments).

Continue past **San Cristobo do Real** R (**27km**, 608m) (albergue), Lusio L, **Renche** R (**28.5km**, 604m) and **San do Martiño Real** R. Follow road past San Julián Benedictine monastery L into **Samos** (**32.5km**, 540m) (accommodation, albergue, refreshments, tourist office).

SAN JULIÁN MONASTERY

Huge murals line the cloisters of the monastery in Samos

The active monastery of San Julián at Samos (pop 200) was founded in the sixth century. Abandoned during the Moorish occupation, it was subsequently repopulated with monks and became a Benedictine house in AD960. As an important stopover on the Camino, it was taken over by monks in communion with Cluny in the 12th century. In 1558 the original building was destroyed by fire and completely rebuilt. The monks were expelled when monasteries were suppressed in 1836, but the Benedictines returned in 1880. Another disastrous fire in 1951 caused much damage and the abbey had to be rebuilt again, this time matching the previous design but with extensive modern murals around the upper gallery. The result of all this rebuilding is a mixture of Gothic, Renaissance and Baroque styles with modern interior decoration. The most spectacular part, the Grand Cloister, is the largest monastic cloister in Spain. The monastery can be visited on guided tours (and you can stay in the monastery's albergue!).

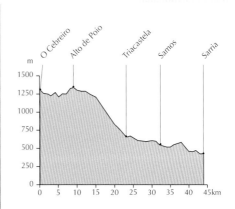

Continue on LU-633 past Foxos, then bear R to pass through **Teiguin** (**34.5km**, 523m) (albergue, refreshments), rejoining main road after village. After 500 metres, fork R again to cross old bridge over río Sarria at Pontenova (refreshments), then rejoin main road. Continue through **Aián** (**38.5km**, 557m). Cross bridge over río Sarria and continue past **Fontao** to reach beginning of Sarria.

Go ahead over mini-roundabout then turn second L (Rúa Mestre Saavedra). Bear L, then turn R to reach roundabout in Plaza de Galicia. Fork R (Rúa do Peregrino, first exit) through housing development to cross Puente Riviera bridge over río Sarria. Turn R at T-junction (Rúa Beningo Quiroga) and after 40 metres turn L (Rúa Arrabaldo) through bollards to reach end of stage at bottom of Escalinata Maior steps in **Sarria** (**44.5km**, 437m) (accommodation, albergue, refreshments, camping, tourist office, cycle shop, station).

STAGE 16
Sarria to Palas de Rei

Start	Sarria, Escalinata Maior steps (437m)
Finish	Palas de Rei town hall (553m)
Distance	47km; road route 47.5km
Ascent	943m; road route 914m
Descent	827m; road route 798m

This stage follows a mixture of shaded lanes and quiet roads passing a string of tiny hamlets, undulating through the low mountains of Galicia. Two ridges are crossed as the route ascends from Sarria over the Serra do Páramo, descends to Portomarín in the Miño valley then climbs over Serra de Ligonde before descending to Palas de Rei. The road route follows the LU-633 for the first half through Portomarín, then an unnumbered minor road to reach Palas de Rei.

Camino route

From bottom of Escalinata Maior steps in **Sarria**, cycle N along cobbled street and turn L uphill at end (Rúa Marqués de Ugena). ▶ Turn first L (Rúa Maior), continuing to ascend, and bear R opposite top of steps. Continue past Santa Mariña church R up street lined with pilgrim albergues. Turn R opposite San Salvador church (Rúa do Castelo), ascending past Miradoiro do Cáceres with views over Sarria R. Just before entrance to Magdalena monastery R, turn L steeply downhill (sp Barbadelo) and pass cemetery R. At T-junction, turn R into open country and after 200 metres, turn L on stone bridge over río Celeiro. Bear L beside railway then follow gravel track winding through fields and passing under motorway viaduct high above. Go ahead over railway crossing and turn L beside railway. Cross stream and bear R ascending steeply through woods, then turn sharply L and follow

The walkers' Camino goes up the steps; the route described here avoids the need to carry your cycle up the steps.

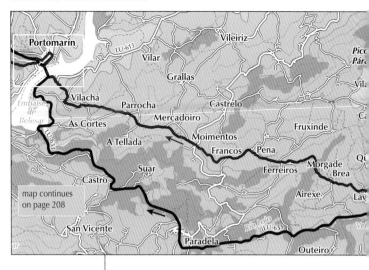

track winding through fields. Turn R by farm then emerge on road and bear L into **Vilei** (**4km**, 522m) (accommodation, albergue, refreshments).

Bear R in village then after leaving village fork R and turn R opposite entrance to 12th-century church and ruins of **Barbadelo abbey** (accommodation, albergue). ◄ Fork L off road through **Rente** (**5.5km**, 594m) (albergue), bearing R in hamlet to return to road. Continue uphill to **A Serra** (**6.5km**, 630m) (albergue, refreshments) and dogleg L and R onto gravel track past farm. Continue through woodland and fields to reach junction of tracks by large fountain. Turn L, then continue to reach gateway to mill L decorated with millstones and turn R. Drop down to cross stone causeway over small stream, then cross LU-633 main road and follow rural road ahead, curving L and continuing to **Peruscallo** (**9km**, 632m).

Pass through village and where road ends, continue ahead on track that winds through forest to Cortiñas and continues to **Lavandeira**. Dogleg R and L across quiet road then continue winding through fields, crossing another stream by stone causeway, to reach road at **Brea**

Barbadelo was a mixed convent of nuns and monks under the control of Samos monastery.

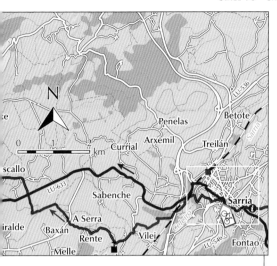

(**11.5km**, 660m). Turn R through hamlet and continue on road to **Morgade** (albergue, refreshments), where road ends. Continue ahead on track winding through fields.

Seasonal ford and causeway near Marzán

Where path ends, dogleg R and L onto start of road and follow this past **Ferreiros** L (**13.5km**, 659m) (albergue, refreshments).

By carpark for restaurant, turn L and immediately R, downhill past church and roadside cemetery in Mirallos (refreshments). Continue on road, then fork L on gravel track. At beginning of **Pena** (**14.5km**, 644m) (albergue), turn R uphill to rejoin road and follow this, forking L downhill at end of village. Continue on road through **Francos** (**15km**, 638m) (albergue, refreshments), then fork R on gravel track into trees. Soon start

The bridge over the Embalse de Belesar leading to Portomarín

descending steadily to reach crossroads and continue ahead on track into **Moimentos** (**16.5km**, 582m). Bear R onto road, then soon after village fork L on gravel track downhill to **Mercadoiro** (**17km**, 537m) (accommodation, albergue, refreshments).

Continue through Moutrás to reach road and bear L. Where road turns R at road junction, turn L (sp A Tellada) and immediately R on track downhill. Emerge beside road R and bear L to pass through **Parrocha** (**19km**, 487m) (refreshments). Join road after village and bear L, then after 175 metres fork R on gravel track through fields. Go ahead over road into **Vilachá** (**20km**, 425m) (albergue, refreshments). Pass through centre of village and continue through fields. Follow road bearing R, then go ahead over staggered crossroads. ▶ Fork L downhill to reach LU-613 main road on apex of hairpin bend. Turn L and follow road downhill to road junction beside bridge. Turn R (LU-633) over **Embalse de Belesar reservoir** and R at roundabout at far end of bridge (first exit, sp Portomarín). ▶ Turn first L (sp Centro) and third L on arcaded Rúa Fraga Inbarne through centre of **Portomarín** (**22.5km**, 387m) (accommodation, albergue, refreshments, tourist office, cycle shop).

Ignore Camino waymarks pointing left as this route is unsuitable for cycles.

To bypass Portomarín, turn L at roundabout (second exit) beside lake L, then turn L over next bridge to regain route.

When the Belesar dam was built across the río Miño in 1962, the old town of **Portomarín** (modern-day pop 1500) disappeared beneath the waters of the reservoir behind the dam. Some of the principal buildings, including the Romanesque San Xoán church, were taken down brick-by-brick and re-erected on Monte do Cristo overlooking the lake, to form the nucleus of a new town. During dry periods, when the water falls to a low level, some of the old buildings and the old bridge are exposed above the water.

Continue through town, bearing R (Rúa Chantada) and dropping

207

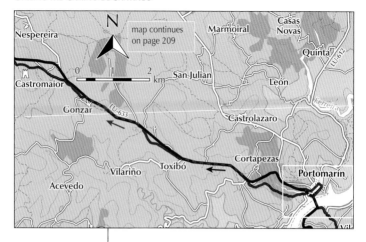

down towards lake. Turn sharply back L (sp Paradela) on LU-633 and turn R (sp Pombal) over lake on first bridge. At far end of bridge turn R on quiet road and where it ends continue on track ascending through forest. Emerge beside LU-633 main road then follow senda L, soon crossing to R of road and continuing to **Toxibó** (**27km**, 491m). By turn L for Vilariño, fork L on gravel track winding through woods beside main road, eventually returning to road and continuing to **Gonzar** (**30km**, 549m) (albergue, refreshments).

Shortly after village, fork L on track and bear R to wind through woods parallel with road. Emerge on road and turn L through **Castromaior** (**31.5km**, 601m) (accommodation, albergue, refreshments). After village fork L (sp Castro de Castromaior) steeply uphill, then fork R on gravel track past ruins of Iron Age fort L. ◀ At top of hill turn R to return to main road. Bear L on senda R and after 500 metres, fork L to pass through **Hospital da Cruz** (**33.5km**, 681m) (albergue, refreshments). At end of village, bear R then turn L across road bridge, using cycle track L. Turn L down slip road on opposite side and fork R on rural road. Just before **Ventas do Narón** (**35.5km**, 703m) (albergue, refreshments), fork L on sunken lane

Castromaior castle was a fourth-century BC hilltop camp with three rings of fortification that was later reused by the Romans.

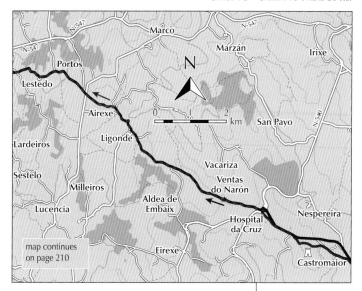

to pass through village centre, rejoining road at end of village. Follow road ascending to soon reach unmarked summit (725m) at Alto de Ligonde, then descend past A Previsa (refreshments) and Os Lameiros to reach **Ligonde** (**38km**, 631m) (albergue).

After village, continue on road descending around hairpin bend. ▶ Continue to **Airexe** (**39.5km**, 627m) (accommodation, albergue, refreshments). Fork L in village then go ahead over crossroads (sp Lestedo) and continue through **Portos** (**41.5km**, 583m) (albergue), **Lestedo** (albergue) and **Os Valos** (**43km**, 635m) to **A Brea** (**44km**, 621m) (albergue, refreshments).

Where rural road bears R to join N-547 main road, fork L past Mesón A Brea inn R, onto gravel track and follow this at first through fields then beside main road. Fork L on stone paved road beside bus stop through **Rosario** (**45km**, 627m) (albergue, refreshments) and continue through fields and forest to reach road on outskirts of Palas de Rei. Turn R (Rúa de Cruceiro), then continue

Ignore Camino signs pointing left which follow a narrow rocky descent unsuitable for cycles.

209

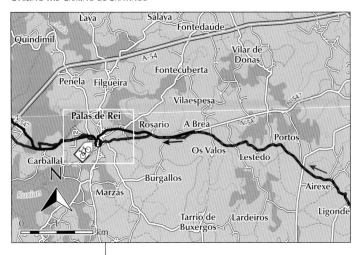

Ignore a Camino sign pointing left off Rúa de Cruceiro which takes a route down stairs.

to main road and turn sharply L downhill. ◀ After 50 metres, turn R before building 24 down ramp beside stairs and through narrow alleyway to reach main road again opposite town hall in **Palas de Rei** (**47km**, 553m) (accommodation, albergue, refreshments, camping, tourist office, cycle shop).

Palas de Rei (pop 3500) is a small town with little of interest. In recent years it has suffered from prolonged rural depopulation as the number of residents has fallen from 13,000 (1940) to 3500 (2016).

Road route

From bottom of Escalinata Maior steps in **Sarria**, cycle N along cobbled pedestrian street and turn L at end (Rúa Marqués de Ugena, LU-633). Where this becomes no entry, fork L steeply uphill then fork R (Rúa Fray Luis de Granada). Drop down then up again, then bear R (Rúa Calexa) downhill and turn L at traffic lights (Rúa San

Lázaro, LU-633). Continue over río Celeiro and railway bridge to roundabout. Turn L (LU-633, third exit, sp Paradela) and ascend on main road through fields and patches of woodland to first summit (**6km**, 621m). Descend, then rise again through **Paradela** (**15km**, 609m) (refreshments) to second summit (**16.5km**, 644m). Descend steeply to shore of **Embalse de Belesar reservoir**, then cross río Loio (sidearm of reservoir) (accommodation, refreshments) and continue winding above shoreline to reach Portomarín bridge. Turn L over río Miño to **Portomarín** (**23.5km**, 350m) (accommodation, albergue, refreshments, tourist office, cycle shop). ▸

San Xoán church in Portomarín was rebuilt on higher ground above the waters of the Belesar reservoir

To visit Portomarín centre, turn R uphill at roundabout following sp Centro.

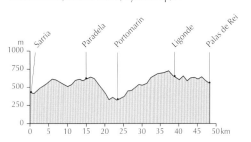

Turn L at roundabout (LU-633, second exit, sp Alto do Hospital) and follow main road beside lake L. At top of first rise, keep L beside mini roundabout (sp Alto do Hospital) and cross bridge over río Barrela. Ascend steadily past **Toxibó** (**28km**, 491m) and **Gonzar** (**31km**, 549m) (albergue, refreshments) to reach motorway junction (**34.5km**, 690m) where LU-633 ends. Cross bridge over motorway (sp Ventas) then turn L and R halfway down slip road (sp Ventas do Narón). Continue ascending past **Ventas do Narón** (**36km**, 703m) (albergue, refreshments) and over summit at Alto de Ligonde (725m). Descend past A Previsa and Os Lameiros to reach **Ligonde** (**39km**, 631m) (albergue).

Fork L in **Airexe** (**40km**, 627m) (albergue, refreshments) and continue past **Portos** (**42km**, 583m) (albergue), **Lestedo** (albergue), **Os Valos** (**43.5km**, 635m) and **A Brea** (**45km**, 621m) (albergue, refreshments). Fork R in front of Mesón A Brea inn, then bear L onto N-547 main road and follow this downhill through **Rosario** (albergue, refreshments) into **Palas de Rei** (**47.5km**, 553m) (accommodation, albergue, refreshments, camping, tourist office, cycle shop).

Palas de Rei town hall

STAGE 17

Palas de Rei to Arzúa

Start	Palas de Rei town hall (553m)
Finish	Arzúa, tourist office (389m)
Distance	28km; road route 29.5km
Ascent	431m; road route 460m
Descent	595m; road route 624m

Continuing to undulate through the green hills of Galicia, this short stage goes through an area of cattle and dairy farms, interspersed by eucalyptus woodland. Midway the regional centre of Melide is passed. The road route follows the N-547 throughout.

Camino route

Follow road R of town hall in **Palas de Rei** (Travesía del Peregrino) W. Turn R at end and after 30 metres, fork L (Rúa do Apostolo) steeply downhill on stone slab path. Turn R at T-junction and continue across main road (Ruá do río Roxan) to reach T-junction. Turn L on quiet road,

map continues on page 216

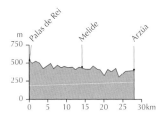

then fork L beside pilgrim monument to return to main road. Bear R, passing industrial estate L, then fork R onto lay-by on track of old road. Return to main road and after 50 metres fork R on gravel track climbing steeply through **Carballal** (**1.5km**, 533m).

After village follow track curving L in woods and return to main road. Cross road and turn R on senda. After 100 metres, fork L into layby and L again on rough sunken track into woods. Bear R on quiet road and after 50 metres turn L to pass under motorway then continue

Stone horreos (granaries), like these at San Xulián, are common in Galicia

to **San Xulián** (**3km**, 464m) (albergue). Turn L then pass church L and continue through fields and over crossroads through A Graña. Descend steeply on sunken track to emerge on road and bear L, then cross río Pambre into Ponte Campaña (albergue, refreshments) and fork R on gravel track. Continue through fields and forest to emerge on road and continue ahead to **Casanova** (**5.5km**, 481m) (albergue, refreshments).

Cycle uphill through hamlet, then fork R at first junction and L at second onto track downhill through forest. Cross small stream then emerge on road in **Campanilla** (refreshments) and bear R to reach O Coto (**8km**, 479m) (albergue, refreshments). Bear L on main street through village, then after 75 metres, fork L on gravel track through woods and go ahead into **O Leboreiro** (**9km**, 450m) (accommodation).

Continue through village then go ahead on track and cross río Seco on 12th-century stone arch bridge. Emerge on narrow road and bear R, then after 125 metres fork L on tree-lined gravel track. Fork L again to follow track

A wayside cross in O Leboreiro

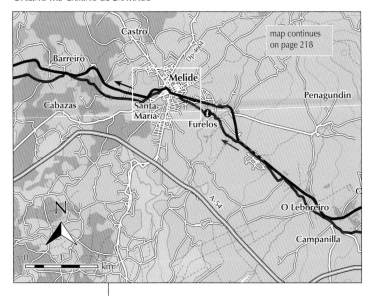

map continues on page 218

winding through fields and woodland with N-547 road R. Pass industrial estate L and continue beside N-547, then bear L away from N-547. Emerge on rural road and continue ahead for 250 metres then fork R downhill on track through woods. Turn L to reach medieval bridge over río Furelos and turn R across bridge into **Furelos** (**13km**, 409m) (albergue, refreshments, tourist office).

Bear L through village, passing church R. Turn L, then at end of village go ahead over staggered crossroads and fork R through fields. Emerge on residential road, then go ahead over crossroads on stone block track and fork R to reach N-547 main road. Bear L to reach mini-roundabout and turn R (Ronda da Coruña, first exit) then fork L (Rúa do Convento) to reach Praza do Convento in front of town hall in **Melide** (**14.5km**, 456m) (accommodation, albergue, refreshments, cycle shop).

Melide (pop 7500) is the centre of an agricultural area known for the quality of its beef and dairy products, with a cattle market on the last Sunday of each month. Despite being well inland, the town is also renowned for its octopus (*pulpe*). As the last major stopover on the medieval Camino, it was well supplied with churches and monastic institutions including Romanesque-style San Roque (formerly San Pedro) and Santa María. Sancti Spiritus was formerly a Franciscan monastery and has an important Baroque altarpiece. The 18th-century Carme chapel is brightly decorated.

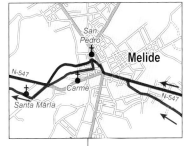

Turn L in plaza into Rúa Camiño de Oviedo. Continue into Rúa Nova and turn R at crossroads (Rúa San Pedro). Follow this out of town ascending past Carme chapel and cemetery (both L). Continue steeply downhill on rough track then turn R onto main road and immediately L (sp Visantoña). After 225 metres, turn R on concrete road through Santa María hamlet. Pass wayside cross L, then

Bikes need to be carried over the río Catasol clapper bridge

fork L onto country lane that winds through fields past series of farms. Where road bears L, keep ahead R on sunken lane through woods. Cross río Catasol by walking cycle over series of slabs that make up narrow stone clapper bridge. ◄ Continue to T-junction and turn R to reach main road. Follow senda L of road for 150 metres and turn L on narrow lane into woods. Emerge onto quiet road and follow this for 225 metres. Where road bears L, continue ahead on gravel track through woods. Cross bridge then emerge onto country lane and follow this winding past series of farms and through **A Peroxa** hamlet (refreshments) into **Boente** (**20km**, 398m) (albergue, refreshments).

Follow road winding through village and bear L by fountain beside main road. Turn R beside church R on stone block track. Bear L through fields and woods then dogleg across quiet road. Drop down steeply to pass under main road and cross stream then ascend very steeply on track winding through woodland. Emerge onto quiet road and continue ahead to reach **Castañeda** (**22.5km**, 414m) (albergue, refreshments).

At beginning of hamlet fork L (sp Río) then keep R at road junction. Continue between fields and through **Río** hamlet downhill to reach triangular junction. Fork L then continue uphill ahead over crossroads and into woodland. Follow road turning sharply R and continue

The bridge crossing is very tricky. There is an alternative ford, but you may need to remove panniers and carry your cycle and bags across the bridge separately.

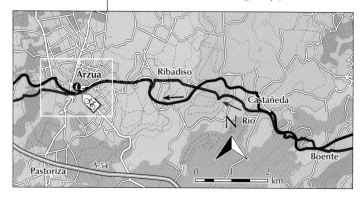

over road bridge. Dogleg over road junction then continue downhill over río Iso into **Ribadiso** (**25.5km**, 306m) (accommodation, albergue, refreshments).

Cycle through village and ascend to T-junction. Turn L then L again beside main road. Pass under road bridge and turn sharply R, continuing uphill through Ribadiso de Arriba (albergue). Emerge beside main road (N-547) and continue on senda L into **Arzúa** (**28km**, 389m) (accommodation, albergue, refreshments, camping, tourist office, cycle shop) then descend to reach end of stage at road junction beside tourist office.

> The mostly modern town of **Arzúa** (pop 6250) sits at the centre of a dairy farming area (the surrounding district is said to have more cows than people) and is known for producing Ulloa, a cylindrically shaped soft creamy cows' cheese. A cheese festival is held every March.

Road route

From town hall in **Palas de Rei**, follow N-547 main road (sp Melide) winding through town centre and continue downhill through **Carballal** (**1.5km**, 513m) and under motorway junction. Descend through **San Pedro Meixide** (**4km**, 458m) and cross río Pambre, then ascend through Saa and follow road undulating through Corral de Riba

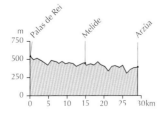

and O Coto (**8.5km**, 479m) (accommodation, albergue, refreshments).

Continue on N-547, passing industrial estate L and crossing río Furelos, then ascend to reach mini-roundabout in centre of Melide. Turn R (Ronda da Coruña, first exit) then fork L (Rúa do Convento) to reach Praza do Convento in front of town hall in **Melide** (15km, 457m) (accommodation, albergue, refreshments, cycle shop).

From plaza, follow Rúa San Antonio L of town hall and continue out of town descending on Rúa de Sabián to reach crossroads. Turn R (N-547, sp Santiago) onto main road and follow this over low ridge, then descend through **Boente** (**20.5km**, 398m) (albergue, refreshments). Cross río Boente then ascend using climbing lane R. Pass under road bridge then turn L (sp Castañeda) at top of hill onto side road. Turn R at T-junction and follow road through **Castañeda** (**23km**, 414m) (albergue, refreshments).

At end of village, bear R under bridge then turn L to rejoin N-547 main road. Descend to cross río Iso then 400 metres after river bridge, bear L onto parallel asphalt road. Follow this ascending through **Ribadiso** (**27.5km**, 350m) (albergue) and rejoin N-547 after village. Continue ascending, then descend to reach end of stage at road junction beside tourist office L in **Arzúa** (**29.5km**, 389m) (accommodation, albergue, refreshments, camping, tourist office, cycle shop).

Arzúa

STAGE 18
Arzúa to Santiago de Compostela

Start	Arzúa, tourist office (389m)
Finish	Santiago de Compostela cathedral (259m)
Distance	38.5km; road route 39km
Ascent	739m; road route 566m
Descent	869m; road route 696m

This final stage undulates through the dairy farms and eucalyptus plantations that dot the green hills of Galicia using a mixture of field paths, narrow lanes and rural roads. At Monte do Gozo, Santiago comes into sight, after which city streets are followed to finish in front of the cathedral. The road route alternative follows the N-547 throughout.

Camino route
From road junction in centre of **Arzúa** follow Rúa Cima do Lugar (L of tourist office) downhill. Continue ahead into Rúa do Carme then fork L beside small pilgrims' cross. Continue downhill on narrow track through fields to As Barrosas hamlet then continue winding through woodland to cross río Brandeso. Climb uphill then bear L on quiet road and fork R through **Preguntoño**

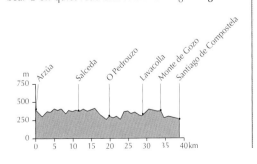

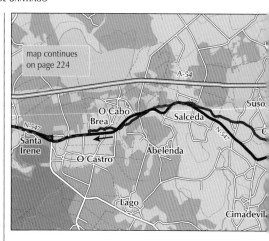

(refreshments). Dogleg R and L onto gravel track uphill. Pass under main road and continue uphill through fields. Dogleg R and L over crossroads and fork L in **A Peroxa** (refreshments). Follow track winding through woodland then go ahead at crossroads and ahead again over motorway (albergue, refreshments). Fork R downhill to reach **A Calzada** (**6.5km**, 388m) (refreshments).

Pass through edge of village then go ahead at crossroads. Continue through commercial forest and fields. Emerge on road, then immediately fork L behind farm building and continue into **Outeiro** (**8km**, 347m) (accommodation, refreshments). At beginning of village, fork R on stone block track and where it ends continue on asphalt road. After 30 metres fork L then after 80 metres turn R on narrow track. ◀ Dogleg L and R over quiet road onto narrow track beside barn. At end of village rejoin road then fork immediately R on gravel track. Go ahead over crossroads and continue past commercial woodland. Go ahead over next crossroads then after 100 metres fork L on gravel track to Boavista hamlet (refreshments). Go ahead on asphalt road then dogleg L and R over crossroads. Bear L on asphalt road then go ahead over crossroads onto sunken lane through woods. Dogleg

The track can be muddy when wet.

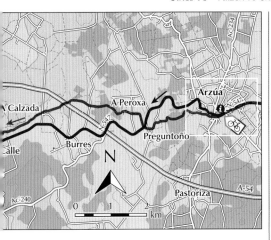

R and L over next crossroads then fork L on gravel track and bear R on senda through **Salceda** (**11.5km**, 362m) (accommodation, albergue, refreshments).

Fork R away from main road on gravel track through woods, returning to main road after 600 metres. Pass tractor sales depot R then cross road and fork L through woods. Go ahead over two crossroads then pass through Ras hamlet. Drop down to pass under main road and continue away from road on gravel track opposite to reach **Brea** (**13.5km**, 375m) (accommodation, albergue, refreshments).

Bear L on road then turn R on gravel track beside house 26. Fork L at track junction then bear L on asphalt road and turn L at T-junction to reach main road. Turn R on senda, then after 400 metres cross main road and continue on other side to Empalme (albergue, refreshments). Re-cross main road at road junction then turn R beside bus shelter away from road. ▸ Continue to reach woods and turn L beside woodland and follow track back to road. Continue beside main road passing through lay-by (albergue, refreshments), eventually forking R on gravel track away from road downhill through forest. Cross side road, then drop down to pass under main road. Follow

The right turn is easy to miss.

223

minor road ahead for 150 metres, then fork R on gravel track through woodland to reach **A Rúa** (**18km**, 278m) (accommodation, albergue, refreshments).

Go ahead on asphalt road through village and fork R to reach main road. Dogleg L and R across main road and go ahead on gravel track uphill through woods. Emerge on asphalt road (Rúa Peregrino) and go ahead to T-junction on edge of **O Pedrouzo** (**19.5km**, 291m) (accommodation, albergue, refreshments, tourist office). Turn R (Rúa Concello) and after 150 metres, turn L on gravel track into woods. Emerge on road and turn R then L after 35 metres. Where road bears L, continue ahead on gravel road through forest. At end of trees, turn L and R between fields. Emerge on asphalt road then continue to T-junction and turn R. Turn R again at next T-junction, then fork L and drop down L to pass under N-547 main road in **Amenal** (**22.5km**, 253m) (accommodation, refreshments).

Continue across side road and go ahead on gravel track winding through forest. Turn R at T-junction and continue through forest. Immediately before bridge over motorway, turn L on gravel track past end of **Santiago airport** runway and follow this bearing L parallel with runway. Follow track R across road then turn R (sp San Paio)

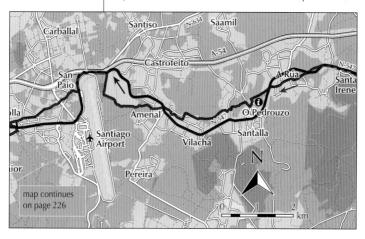

map continues on page 226

on road winding past **San Paio** (**26.5km**, 335m) (refreshments) into forest. Fork L uphill on asphalt track, then fork R on gravel track through forest. Pass under main road and continue ahead on forest track. Fork L at path junction and continue to reach road. Bear R, following road ahead over crossroads into **Lavacolla** (**28.5km**, 297m) (accommodation, albergue, refreshments). ▸

Fork L then turn L and R past church L winding through village. Continue across main road (sp Vilamaior). After 100 metres, turn sharply R to cross río Sionlla on small wooden bridge, then turn R along road. Continue through forest to **Vilamaior** (**30km**, 354m) (accommodation, refreshments). Fork L and turn R in village, then continue through forest passing studios of TV Galicia (regional TV company) R. Turn sharply L at T-junction past campsite L (camping) and studios of RTVE Galicia (national TV company) R. ▸ Turn first R and continue through fields to T-junction. Turn R and after 100 metres turn L through **San Marcos** (**33.5km**, 368m) (accommodation, albergue, refreshments, camping, cycle shop).

At end of village cross small ridge with first view of Santiago cathedral in distance ahead and complex of buildings L on **Monte do Gozo**.

Monte do Gozo (380m), which means 'hill of joy', is the last hill on the Camino, rising 70m above the track and 120m above Santiago. It was traditionally the place where pilgrims would break into a run and cry out in rapture at catching a glimpse of the cathedral's triple spires. In 1989 Pope John Paul II led a mass from the top of the hill preaching to an open-air congregation of 250,000 worshippers, an event marked by a modern sculpture on the hilltop. Since then, the hill has been extensively developed with landscaped walks, groves of eucalyptus, concert stage, campsite and a sprawling 500-bed pilgrim hostel to relieve pressure on accommodation in the city. The only remnant of the medieval pilgrimage is the small chapel of San Marcos.

In medieval times, Lavacolla was the place where pilgrims would stop to wash and cleanse themselves before arriving in Santiago.

The road route joins here for the final leg into Santiago.

The extensive pilgrim hostel at Monte do Gozo

Cycle ahead downhill, then where road turns sharply R, continue ahead onto concrete ramp that snakes down hillside. At bottom emerge beside road and continue over motorway and railway bridges using track behind barriers L. Go ahead over three roundabouts then fork

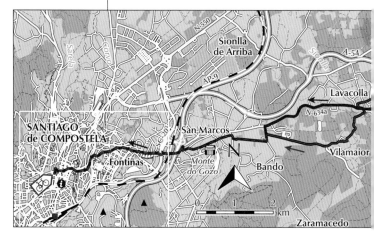

L downhill (Rúa do Valiño) by obelisk-style monument
L. Continue into Rúa das Fontiñas, becoming Rúa da
Fonte Concheiros. Continue ahead over major crossroads
(Rúa dos Concheiros, now cobbles) to reach Cruceiro
San Pedro crossroads. Continue ahead onto Rúa de San
Pedro to reach Porto do Camiño where Camino enters
old city. ▶ Go ahead on pedestrianised Rúa das Casa
Reais winding through old city and bear L into Praza de
Cervantes. Turn R (Rúa da Acibechería) to reach Praza
da Inmaculada by N transept door to cathedral L. Bear R
(Travesa das Dúas Portas), dropping downhill, then turn
L (Rúa de San Francisco) past Hostal dos Reyes Católicos
(now a parador) R to reach Praza do Obradoiro square in
front of cathedral in **Santiago de Compostela** (**38.5km**,
259m) (accommodation, albergue, youth hostel, refreshments, tourist office, cycle shop, station).

This is a one-way
street with cycling
prohibited so
walk your cycle
for 400 metres.

For most modern pilgrims, Santiago cathedral is journey's end, although some choose to continue for a few
more days to reach Cape Finisterre (literally 'the end of
the world') on Galicia's rocky north-west coast. But for
medieval pilgrims, Santiago was only halfway as they
had to turn around and retrace the route for the journey
home. As you head to the station or airport and moan
about late running trains or airline luggage allowances,
just think how much easier your journey is than that of
the peregrinos of old.

SANTIAGO DE COMPOSTELA

The great religious centre of Santiago de Compostela (pop 96,000) had 500
years of prosperity during the medieval pilgrimage followed by 400 years of
dormancy until the mid twentieth century when growth of the modern-day
pilgrimage has brought prosperity back to the city. Within the maze of small
streets that comprise the inner old city are numerous churches, monasteries,
convents and seminaries together with small shops catering to a market of
tourists and pilgrims.At the heart of all this is Praza do Obradoiro (workshop
square, where the stonemasons and carpenters worked during construction
of the cathedral). Three great buildings overlook the square. The Hostal dos
Reyes Católicos was a pilgrim hospital in Plateresque style commissioned

Santiago cathedral: the majestic finish-point of the Camino (photo: Jonathan Williams)

by King Ferdinand and Queen Isabella of Spain in the early 16th century. Later it became the city hospital before conversion in 1954 into a parador (a chain of state-owned hotels in historic buildings) and is one of the great hotels of the world. The neoclassical Palacio de Raxoi is an 18th-century building designed like a French palace. Intended as a seminary, it has had a variety of uses including a prison (the old gaol stood on the same site). Nowadays it houses departments of the regional council. On the pediment looking across the square to the cathedral is a huge statue of Santiago Matamoros (St James the Moor-slayer).

The triple spired cathedral of St James rises above the city, both literally and metaphorically. The remains of St James were originally kept in a small chapel. As the pilgrimage grew, work started (1075) on a cathedral to house the casket and make it accessible for veneration by pilgrims. The initial Romanesque building was extended in Gothic style during the 15th century and in 1740 the Baroque west façade was added. At the rear of the cathedral, the Porta do Perdón (Door of Forgiveness) is opened only during jubilee years. Inside, the Botafumeiro (a very large silver incense burner) is swung from side to

The Botafumeiro is swung after pilgrim mass

side across the transept at the end of pilgrim mass. This is a throwback to the time when the pilgrimage was not as hygienic as it is today. Medieval pilgrims would arrive having not washed for weeks and then sleep on the floor of the cathedral; incense was burned to purify the air. The objective of the pilgrimage, the 'relics' of St James, are housed in the crypt, a fitting place to end your trip. A statue of St James, which many pilgrims wish to embrace, is mounted above the high altar and can be reached by a narrow flight of stone stairs; easy to find, just look for the queue of pilgrims waiting to ascend!

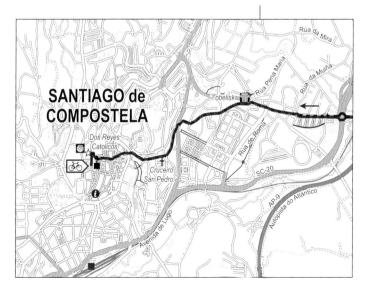

The first view of Santiago cathedral, seen from Monte do Gozo

Road route

From road junction in centre of **Arzúa**, follow N-547 W (R of tourist office), then continue downhill to cross río Brandeso and undulate past new motorway junction. ◄ Continue through **Burres** (**6km**, 377m), **Salceda** (**12.5km**, 371m) (accommodation, albergue, refreshments), **Brea** (**14.5km**, 372m) (accommodation, albergue, refreshments) and Empalme (**16km**, 408m) (albergue, refreshments). Descend steeply past **Santa Irene** L (albergue) and **A Rúa** (**18.5km**, 283m) (accommodation, refreshments) to **O Pedrouzo** (**20km**, 284m) (accommodation, albergue, refreshments, tourist office).

The new motorway under construction when this guide was being written will greatly reduce traffic on the N-547.

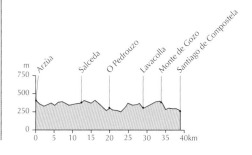

Continue to **Amenal** (**23km**, 249m) (accommodation, refreshments) then ascend steeply through woods to reach roundabout. Turn L (second exit) and follow road bearing L beside motorway. Continue past end of **Santiago airport** runway L then bear L away from motorway on quiet road. Go ahead over next roundabout (N-634, sp Lavacolla) and continue through **Lavacolla** (**29km**, 301m) (accommodation, albergue, refreshments).

Continue on main road and after 3km pass turning L to TV Galicia studios. Take next turn L (sp Vilamaior). Keep R at fork past campsite L (camping) to join camino route. Turn first R and continue through fields to T-junction. Turn R and after 100 metres turn L through **San Marcos** (**33.5km**, 368m) (accommodation, albergue, refreshments, camping, cycle shop). At end of village cross small ridge with first view of Santiago cathedral in distance ahead and complex of buildings L on **Monte do Gozo**.

Cycle ahead downhill, then where road turns sharply R, continue ahead onto concrete ramp that snakes down hillside. At bottom emerge beside road and continue over motorway and railway bridges using track behind barriers L. Go ahead over three roundabouts then fork L downhill (Rúa do Valiño) by obelisk-style monument L. Continue into Rúa das Fontiñas, becoming Rúa da Fonte Concheiros. Continue ahead over major crossroads (Rúa dos Concheiros, now cobbles) to reach Cruceiro San Pedro crossroads. Continue ahead onto Rúa de San Pedro to reach Porto do Camiño where Camino enters old city. ▶ Go ahead on pedestrianised Rúa das Casa Reais winding through old city and bear L into Praza de Cervantes. Turn R (Rúa da Acibecheria) to reach Praza da Inmaculada by N transept door to cathedral L. Bear R (Travesa das Dúas Portas), dropping downhill, then turn L (Rúa de San Francisco) past Hostal dos Reyes Católicos (now a parador) R to reach Praza do Obradoiro square in front of cathedral in **Santiago de Compostela** (**39km**, 259m) (accommodation, albergue, youth hostel, refreshments, tourist office, cycle shop, station).

This is a one-way street with cycling prohibited so walk your cycle for 400 metres.

APPENDIX A
Facilities summary table

Location	Distance	Cumulative	Altitude	Accommodation	Albergue	Refreshments	Camping	Tourist office	Cycle shop	Station
Stage 1										
St Jean-Pied-de-Port	0	0	187	×	×	×	×	×	×	×
Venta Peio						×				
Arnéguy	8.5	8.5	256	×		×				
Valcarlos	3	11.5	367	×	×	×				
Roncesvalles	16.5	28	948	×	×	×		×		
Stage 2										
Burguette	3	31	898	×		×				
Espinal	3.5	34.5	871	×	×	×	×			
Gerendiain	5	39.5	782	×		×				
Lintzoáin	1.5	41	741	×		×				
Zubiri	8	49	532	×	×	×		×		
Ezkirotz					×					
Larrasoaña	5.5	54.5	503	×	×	×				
Akerreta				×						

Location	Distance	Cumulative	Altitude	Accommodation	Albergue	Refreshments	Camping	Tourist office	Cycle shop	Station
Zuriáin	3.5	58	476		×	×				
Irotz	2	60	476			×				
F-uarte	4.5	64.5	445	×	×	×				
Pamplona	6	70.5	457	×	×	×		×	×	×
Stage 3										
Cizur Menor	5	75.5	466		×	×				
Zariquiegui	6	81.5	627		×	×				
Uterga	6	87.5	492		×	×				
Muruzábal	2.5	90	442		×	×				
Obanos	1.5	91.5	414	×	×	×				
Puente la Reina	3	94.5	351	×	×	×	×	×		
Mañeru	4.5	99	454		×	×				
Cirauqui	2.5	101.5	471		×	×				
Lorca	5.5	106.5	463		×	×				
Villatuerta	4.5	111.5	423		×	×				
Estella	4	115.5	423	×	×	×	×	×	×	

Location	Distance	Cumulative	Altitude	Accommodation	Albergue	Refreshments	Camping	Tourist office	Cycle shop	Station
Stage 4										
Ayegui	1.5	117	502		x	x				
Irache	2.5	119.5	564		x		x			
Azqueta	3	122.5	581	x	x	x				
Villamayor de Monjardín	2	124.5	676	x	x	x				
Los Arcos	11	135.5	445	x	x	x				
Sansol	6.5	142	493	x	x	x				
Torres del Río	1	143	464		x	x				
Viana	11.5	154.5	471	x	x	x		x		
Logroño	9.5	164	382	x	x	x	x	x	x	x
Stage 5										
Navarrete	12.5	176.5	513	x	x	x	x	x		
Ventosa	6.5	183	632	x	x	x				
Nájera	10	193	485	x	x	x	x	x	x	
Azofra	6	199	552	x	x	x				
Rio Alto golf club						x				
Cirueña	9.5	208.5	743		x	x				

Location	Distance	Cumulative	Altitude	Accommodation	Albergue	Refreshments	Camping	Tourist office	Cycle shop	Station
Santo Domingo de la Calzada	5.5	214	639	x	x	x		x	x	
Stage 6										
Granón	6.5	220.5	726	x	x	x				
Redecilla del Camino	4	224.5	742	x	x	x		x		
Castildelgado	1.5	226	769	x	x	x				
V loria de R oja	2	228	800	x	x	x				
Villamayor del Río	3.5	231.5	788	x	x	x				
Belorado	4.5	236	769	x	x	x		x		
Tosantos	5	241	821		x	x			x	
Villambista	2	243	860		x	x				
Espinosa del Camino	1.5	244.5	898		x	x				
Villafranca Montes de Oca	3.5	248	944	x	x	x				

Location	Distance	Cumulative	Altitude	Accommodation	Albergue	Refreshments	Camping	Tourist office	Cycle shop	Station
Stage 7										
San Juan de Ortega	12	260	1004		x	x				
Agés	3.5	263.5	968		x	x				
Atapuerca	2.5	266	954		x	x				
Cardeñuela Ríopico	6	272	923		x	x				
Orbaneja Ríopico	2.5	274.5	909		x	x				
Castañares	4.5	279	885			x				
Parque de Fuentes Blancas							x			
Burgos	7.5	286.5	857	x	x	x		x	x	x
Stage 8										
Tardajos	10.5	297	827	x	x	x				
Rabé de las Calzadas	2	299	829		x	x				
Hornillos del Camino	8	307	824	x	x	x				
Hontanas	10.5	317.5	878	x	x	x				

Location	Distance	Cumulative	Altitude	Accommodation	Albergue	Refreshments	Camping	Tourist office	Cycle shop	Station
San Antón					x	x				
Castrojeriz	9	326.5	816	x	x	x	x	x		
Stage 9										
San Nicolás Puentefitero					x					
Itero de la Vega	11	337.5	773	x	x	x				
Boadilla del Camino	8	345.5	783	x	x	x				
Frómista	5.5	351	781	x	x	x		x		x
Población de Campos	4	355	777	x	x	x				
Villarmentero de Campos	5.5	360.5	789	x	x	x				
Villalcázar de Sirga	4	364.5	802	x	x	x				
Carrión de los Condes	5.5	370	838	x	x	x	x	x	x	
Stage 10										
Calzadilla de la Cueza	17	387	857	x	x	x				

Location	Distance	Cumulative	Altitude	Accommodation	Albergue	Refreshments	Camping	Tourist office	Cycle shop	Station
Ledigos	6	393	873	×	×	×				
Terradillos de los Templarios	3	396	877		×	×				
Moratinos	3.5	399.5	860	×	×	×				
San Nicolás del Real Camino	2.5	402	847		×	×				
Sahagún	7	409	835	×	×	×	×	×	×	×
Stage 11										
Bercianos del Real Camino	10.5	419.5	857		×	×				
El Burgo Ranero	7	426.5	880	×	×	×				×
Reliegos	13	439.5	825		×	×				
Mansilla de las Mulas	6	445.5	801	×	×	×	×		×	×
Villamoros de Mansilla	4.5	450	801	×		×				
Villarente	1.5	451.5	801	×	×	×				
Arcahueja	4	455.5	843	×	×	×				
Valdelafuente	1.5	457	867			×				

Location	Distance	Cumulative	Altitude	Accommodation	Albergue	Refreshments	Camping	Tourist office	Cycle shop	Station
Puente del Castro	4.5	461.5	815			x				
León	2.5	464	840	x	x	x	x	x	x	x
Stage 12										
Trobajo del Camino	4	468	841	x		x			x	
La Virgen del Camino	3	471	909	x	x	x				
Valverde de la Virgen	4.5	475.5	891		x	x				
San Miguel del Camino	1.5	477	899			x				
Urbanización Camino de Santiago				x		x				
Villadangos del Páramo	7.5	484.5	899	x	x	x	x			x
San Martín del Camino	4.5	489	869		x	x				
Hospital de Órbigo	7	496	821	x	x	x	x			

Location	Distance	Cumulative	Altitude	Accommodation	Albergue	Refreshments	Camping	Tourist office	Cycle shop	Station
San Justo de la Vega	11.5	507.5	851	×		×				
Astorga	4	511.5	870	×	×	×		×	×	×
Stage 13										
Murias de Rechivaldo	4	515.5	884	×	×	×				
Santa Catalina de Somoza	4.5	520	983		×	×				
El Ganso	4	524	1019		×	×				
Rabanal del Camino	7	531	1158	×	×	×				
Foncebadon	5.5	536.5	1420		×	×				
Manjarin	4.5	541	1441		×					
El Acebo	7	548	1149	×	×	×				
Riego de Ambrós	3.5	551.5	949	×	×	×				
Molinaseca	6	557.5	585	×	×	×		×		
Ponferrada	8	565.5	544	×	×	×		×	×	×
Stage 14										
Columbrianos	5	570.5	526		×	×				

APPENDIX A – FACILITIES SUMMARY TABLE

Location	Distance	Cumulative	Altitude	Accommodation	Albergue	Refreshments	Camping	Tourist office	Cycle shop	Station
Fuentesnuevas	2.5	573	508			x				
Camponaraya	2.5	575.5	493		x	x				
Cacabelos	5.5	581	485	x		x		x	x	
Pieros	2	583	541		x	x				
Valtuille de Arriba	2	585	557	x		x				
Villafranca del Bierzo	4.5	589.5	511	x	x	x	x	x	x	
Pereje	5.5	595	550		x	x				
Trabadelo	4.5	599.5	574		x	x				
La Portela del Valcarce	4	603.5	601	x	x	x				
Ambasmestas	1	604.5	615	x	x	x				
Vega del Valcarce	2.5	607	638	x	x	x				
Ruitelán	1.5	608.5	663		x	x				
Las Herrerías	1	609.5	673	x	x	x				
Hospital	1	610.5	689			x				
La Laguna	6	616.5	1149		x	x				

241

Location	Distance	Cumulative	Altitude	Accommodation	Albergue	Refreshments	Camping	Tourist office	Cycle shop	Station
O Cebreiro	2	618.5	1305	x	x	x				
Stage 15										
Linares	3	621.5	1221		x	x				
Hospital	2.5	624	1242		x	x				
Alto de Poio	3	627	1337	x	x	x				
Fonfría	3.5	630.5	1292		x	x				
O Bibuedo	2	632.5	1185		x	x				
Fillobal	3	635.5	965		x	x				
Triacastela	4	639.5	663	x	x	x				
El Beso					x					
A Balsa	2	641.5	734		x					
Montán	4.5	646	754		x	x				
Furela	3	649	664			x				
Pintín	1	650	630	x		x				
Aguiada	2	652	497		x	x				
San Mamede	1.5	653.5	490		x					
Sarria	3	656.5	437	x	x	x	x	x	x	x
Stage 16										
Vilei	4	660.5	522	x	x	x				

Location	Distance	Cumulative	Altitude	Accommodation	Albergue	Refreshments	Camping	Tourist office	Cycle shop	Station
Barbadelo				X						
Rente	1.5	662	594		X					
A Serra	1	663	630			X				
Morgade					X	X				
Ferreiros	7	670	659		X	X				
Mirallos						X				
Francos	1.5	671.5	638		X	X				
Mercadoiro	2	673.5	537	X	X	X				
Parrocha	2	675.5	487			X				
Vilachá	1	676.5	425		X	X				
Portomarín	2.5	679	387	X	X	X		X	X	
Gonzar	7.5	686.5	549		X	X				
Castromaior	1.5	688	601	X	X	X				
Hospital da Cruz	2	690	681		X	X				
Ventas do Narón	2	692	703		X	X				
A Previsa						X				
Ligonde	2.5	694.5	631		X					

Location	Distance	Cumulative	Altitude	Accommodation	Albergue	Refreshments	Camping	Tourist office	Cycle shop	Station
Airexe	1.5	696	627	x	x	x				
Portos	2	698	583		x					
Lestedo					x					
A Brea	2.5	700.5	621		x	x				
Rosario	1	701.5	627		x	x				
Palas de Rei	2	703.5	553	x	x	x	x	x	x	
Stage 17										
San Xulián	3	706.5	464		x					
Ponte Campaña					x	x				
Casanova	2.5	709	481		x	x				
O Coto	2.5	711.5	479		x	x				
O Leboreiro	1	712.5	450	x		x				
Furelos	4	716.5	409		x	x		x		
Melide	1.5	718	456	x	x	x			x	
A Peroxa						x				
Boente	5.5	723.5	398		x	x				
Castañeda	2.5	726	414		x	x				
Ribadiso	3	729	306	x	x	x				

Location	Distance	Cumulative	Altitude	Accommodation	Albergue	Refreshments	Camping	Tourist office	Cycle shop	Station
Arzúa	2.5	731.5	389	×	×	×	×	×	×	
Stage 18										
Preguntoño						×				
A Peroxa						×				
A Calzada	6.5	738	388			×				
Outeiro	1.5	739.5	347	×		×				
Boavista						×				
Salceda	3.5	743	362	×	×	×				
Brea	2	745	375	×	×	×				
Empalme					×	×				
A Rúa	4.5	749.5	278	×	×	×				
O Pedrouzo	1.5	751	291	×	×	×		×		
Amenal	3	754	253	×		×				
San Paio	4	758	335			×				
Lavacolla	2	760	297	×	×	×				
Vilamaior	1.5	761.5	354	×		×	×			
San Marcos	3.5	765	368	×	×	×	×			
Santiago de Compostela	5	770	259	×	×	×		×	×	×

APPENDIX B
Tourist information offices

Stage 1
St Jean-Pied-de-Port
14 Place Charles de Gaulle
64220
tel +33 559 37 03 57
www.saintjeanpieddeport-paysbasque-
tourisme.com

Roncesvalles
Edificio Antiguo Molino
Calle Roncesvalles
31650
tel +34 948 760 301
www.turismo.navarra.es

Stage 2
Zubiri
Polideportivo Municipal
Avda Roncesvalles 51
31630
tel +34 948 304 797

Pamplona
Calle San Saturnino 2
31001
tel +34 948 420 700
www.turismodepamplona.es

Stage 3
Puente la Reina
Puente de los Pellegrinos 1
31100
tel +34 948 341 301
www.turismo.navarra.es

Estella
Calle San Nicolás 1
31200
tel +34 948 556 301
www.turismo.navarra.es

Stage 4
Los Arcos
Plaza del Coso 2
31210
tel +34 948 640 021
www.losarcos.es/turismo

Viana
Plaza de los Fueros 1
31230
tel +34 948 446 302
www.turismo.navarra.es

Logroño
Calle Portales 50
26071
tel +34 941 291 260
www.lariojaturismo.com

Stage 5
Navarrete
Cuesta El Caño
26370
tel +34 941 440 005
www.navarrete.es/turismo

Nájera
Plaza San Miguel 10
26300
tel +34 941 360 041
www.najeraturismo.es

Santo Domingo de la Calzada
Calle Mayor 33
26250
tel +34 941 341 238
www.santodomingoturismo.es

Stage 6
Redecilla del Camino
El Crucero
09259
tel +34 947 588 004
www.redecilladelcamino.es

Belorado
Plaza Mayor 1
09250
tel +34 947 580 815
www.belorado.es

Stage 7
Burgos
Calle Nuño Rasura 7
09003
tel +34 947 288 874
www.aytoburgos.es/turismo

Stage 8
Castrojeriz
Plaza Mayor 3
09110
tel +34 947 377 001
www.castrojeriz.es/turismo

Stage 9
Frómista
Calle Arquitecto Anibal 2
34440
tel +34 979 810 180
www.fromista.com

Carrión de los Condes
Callejón de Santiago
34120
tel +34 979 880 932
www.carriondeloscondes.org

Stage 10
Sahagún
former Trinidad church
Calle el Arco 87
24320
tel +34 987 781 015
www.villadesahagun.es

Stage 11
León
Plaza de Regla 2
24002
tel +34 987 237 082
www.leon.es

Stage 12
Astorga
Plaza Eduardo de Castro 5
24700
tel +34 987 618 222
www.turismoastorga.es

Stage 13
Molinaseca
Calle Manuel Fraga Iribarne 72
24413
tel +34 987 453 085
http://molinaseca.es

Ponferrada
Calle Gil y Carrasco 4
24400
tel +34 987 424 236
www.ponferrada.org

Stage 14
Cacabelos
Museo Arqueológico
Calle las Angustias 24
24540
tel +34 987 546 993
www.turismocacabelos.org

Villafranca del Bierzo
Ave Diez Ovelar 10
24500
tel +34 987 540 028
www.villafrancadelbierzo.org

Stage 15

Samos
Rúa de Torres
27620
tel +34 982 546 002
www.concellosamos.es

Sarria
Vigo de Sarria 15
27600
tel +34 982 530 099
www.sarriaturismo.com

Stage 16

Portomarín
Caso do Concello
Plaza Conde Fenosa 1
27170
tel +34 982 545 206www.
concellodeportomarin.es

Palas de Rei
Avda de Compostela 28
27100
tel +34 982 380 001
www.concellopalasderei.es

Stage 17

Furelos (Melide)
Casa Museo de Furelos
Rúa Furelos
15809
tel +34 616 137 847
www.turismomelide.com

Arzúa
Plaza do Peregrino
15810
tel +34 981 508 056
www.turismo.concellodearzua.com

Stage 18

O Pedruzo/O Pino
Centro socio-cultural Luis Seoane
Rúa do Peregrino 10
15821
tel +34 981 511 065
www.concellodeopino.com

Santiago de Compostela
Rúa do Vilar 63
15705
tel +34 981 555 129
www.santiagoturismo.com

APPENDIX C
Cycle shops

(B) indicates a member of Bicigrino repair service

Stage 1
Maya Sport (B)
18 Ave de Jai Alai
St Jean-Pied-de-Port
64220
tel +33 5 59 37 15 98
www.mayasport.fr

Stage 2
Vendebicis
Calle Mayor Kale Nagusia 58
Burlada
31600
tel + 34 948 238 971
https://vendebicis.com

Mundoraintxe (B)
Calle Nueva 121
Pamplona
31001
tel + 34 948 213 033
www.mundoraintxe.com

Pedalier
Pl Blanca de Navarra 4
Pamplona
31001
tel + 34 948 244 662
https://pedalier.es

Ciclos Goñi
Calle de Amaya 23
Pamplona
31004
tel + 34 948 232 183

Ciclos Goñi
Calle Erletokieta 8
Pamplona
31007
tel + 34 948 267 247

Bicimarket
Calle Pedro 1
Pamplona
31007
tel + 34 948 591 329
www.bicimarket.com/pamplona

Ciclos Martin
Calle Esquiroz 20
Pamplona
31007
tel + 34 948 276 209
www.ciclosmartin.com

Ciclos Martin
Calle Ermitagaña 5
Pamplona
31008
tel + 34 948 173 834
www.ciclosmartin.com

Stage 3
Bicicletas Lisarri (B)
Paseo de la Inmaculada 56
Estella
31200
tel + 34 696 291 903

Ciclos Lizarra (B)
Calle Fray Diego 38
Estella
31200
tel + 34 948 550 164
www.cicloslizarra.com

Stage 4
Vini Vidi Bici
Paseo Francisco Saenz Porres1
Parque de San Antonio
Logroño
26001
tel + 34 941 257 021
www.vinividibici.com

Bicicletas José Mari
Calle General de Rey 51
Logroño
26002
tel + 34 941 242 414
www.bicicletasjosemari.com

Hogar Ciclos (B)
Calle Gral Vara de Rey 51
Logroño
26003
tel + 34 941 261 236
www.hogarciclos.com

Passion Cycling
Calle Arquitectos Álamo y Ceballos 9
Logroño
26006
tel + 34 941 048 310

Rioja Bicycle Sport
Calle Chile 24
Logroño
26005
tel + 34 941 209 449
www.bicicletasriojasport.es

Ciclosport
Calle Duques de Nájera 16
Logroño
26002
+34 941 261 234
www.ciclosportplus.com

Rollerbike
Avda Club Deportivo 49
Logroño
26007
tel + 34 941 289 503
https://rollerbike.es

Stage 5
Ciclos Baños (B)
Poligono La Pedregosa
Calle Los Álamos 11
Nájera
26300
tel + 34 941 363 482
https://bicicletasyjardineria.com

Demanda Ciclos (B)
Calle San Roque 24 (Avda Cuerpos de
Obras Publicos 1)
Santo Domingo de la Calzada
26250
tel + 34 941 340 011
www.demandaciclos.com

Stage 6
El Salto (repair service) (B)
Camino de los Cauces s/n
Belorado
09250
tel + 34 947 415 639
www.elsalto.eu

Stage 7
Mi Bici-O
Carretera de Poza 103
Burgos
09007
tel + 34 947 274 129
www.mibici-o.com

BikeXtrem
Calle Vitoria 258
Burgos
09007
tel + 34 947 240 003
www.bikextrem.com

Bicicool
Calle Francisco Grandmontagne 23
Burgos
09007
tel + 34 947 063 710

JG Bikes
Calle Obdulio Fernández 14
Burgos
09006
tel + 34 947 260 253
www.jgbikes.es

Mas Bici
Plaza Francisco Sarmiento
Burgos
09005
tel + 34 947 218 295
www.masbiciburgos.com

Velobur (B)
Avda de la Paz 7
Burgos
09004
tel + 34 947 211 303
www.velobur.es

Ciclos Fuentecillas
Calle Murcia 1
Burgos
09003
tel + 34 947 652 552
https://ciclosfuentecillas.blogspot.com

Stage 9
Talleres Juanito (repair service) (B)
Calle Las Cercas 1
Carrión de los Condes
34120
tel + 34 979 880 340

Stage 10
Garaje Redondo (B)
Calle Flora Flórez 18
Sahagún
24320
tel + 34 987 780 013

Stage 11
Delesla (Jesús Gonzales Robles) (B)
Calle de las Mesones 27
Mansilla de las Mulas
24210
tel + 34 987 310 104

Bicicletas Vicente
Calle Fray Luis de León 9
León
24005
tel + 34 987 257 446
www.bicicletasvicente.com

Bicicletas Blanco (B)
Calle Teniente Andrés González 1
León
24005
tel + 34 987 209 610
www.bicicletasblanco.com

Bike León
Calle Conde Guillén 11
León
24004
tel + 34 987 260 257
www.bikeleon.com

Bicicletas Carlos
Calle la Torre 8
León
24002
tel + 34 987 226 022
www.bicicletascarlos.es

Robles Bicicletas (B)
Calle Juan Madrazo 9
León
24002
tel + 34 987 233 219
www.roblesbicicletas.com

Bicicletas Ramón
Calle Federico Echevarria 13
León
24002
tel + 34 987 276 276

Stage 12
Ciclos César
Calle Azorin 13
Trobajo del Camino
24010
tel + 34 987 231 699
www.cicloscesar.com

244Bikes
Avda del Párroco Pablo Diez 244
Trobajo del Camino
24010
tel + 34 987 804 013
https://244bikestore.com

Liebana Bike (B)
Calle del Pozo 4
Astorga
24700
tel + 34 987 616 927
www.liebanabike.es

HT Sport
Calle Santiago Crespo 26
Astorga
24700
tel + 34 987 602 768

Stage 13
Ciclotech
Avda del Castillo 128
Ponferrada
24401
tel + 34 987 032 394

Bici Zona Elite
Calle Ortega y Gasset 27
Ponferrada
24402
tel + 34 987 403 803
www.bicizonaelite.com

Bici Bierzo
Calle San Cristóbal 5
Ponferrada
24402
tel + 34 987 429 828
https://bicibierzo.com

Pedales Bici
Avda Compostilla 8
Ponferrada
24402
tel + 34 987 405 767

Inercia Ponferrada (B)
Calle Gral Gómez Núñez 40
Ponferrada
24400
tel + 34 987 021 116
www.inerciaponferrada.com

Stage 14
Bicis Paco
Calle Ponferrada 10
Cacabelos
24540
tel + 34 600 523 415

Bicibelos (B)
Plaza Mayor 11
Cacabelos
24540
tel + 34 606 663 696

Ciclos Urbano (B)
Calle Puente Nuevo 2
Villafranca del Bierzo
24500
tel + 34 987 540 412
www.motosurbano.com

Stage 15
Dos Ruedas (B)
Praza de Galicia 41
Sarria
27600
tel + 34 982 533 522

Stage 16

Porto Bike
Rúa Compostela 5
Portomarín
27170

Recambios Freire
Avda de Lugo s/n
Palas de Rei
27200
tel + 34 982 380 065
www.recambiosfreire.com

Stage 17
Leiva
Ronda A Coruña 52
Melide
15800
tel + 34 981 507 334

Motos y Bicicletas Isidru
Avda de Lugo 14
Melide
15800
tel + 34 981 505 203

Lamas Bike (B)
Rúa Lugo 131
Arzúa
15810
tel + 34 981 508 013

Stage 18
Bici Total
Cuesta de San Marcos 9
San Marcos
15820
tel + 34 981 564 562
www.bicitotal.es

Velocipedo Bicicletas
Rúa de San Pedro 23
Santiago de Compostela
15703
tel + 34 981 580 260
www.elvelocipedo.com

Bicicletas Oliveira
Rúa de Sánchez Freire 83
Santiago de Compostela
15706
tel + 34 981 523 306

APPENDIX D
Pilgrim information

St Jean-Pied-de-Port
Les Amis du Chemin de St Jacques
39 Rue de la Citadelle
64220
tel +33 5 59 37 05 09
www.aucoeurduchemin.org

Santiago de Compostela
Pilgrim Reception Office
33 Rúa das Carretas
15705
tel +34 981 568 846
https://oficinadelperegrino.com

Pilgrim associations
UK
Confraternity of Saint James
www.csj.org.uk

Australia
Australian Friends of the Camino
www.afotc.org

Brazil
Caminho de Santiago
www.caminhodesantiago.com.br

Canada
The Canadian Company of Pilgrims
www.santiago.ca

France
Société des Amis de Saint Jacques de
Compostela
www.compostelle.asso.fr

Germany
Sankt-Jakobus Gesellschaft
https://deutsche-jakobus-gesellschaft.de

Ireland
Camino Society Ireland
www.caminosociety.com

Netherlands
Het Nederlands Genootschap van Sint
Jacob
www.santiago.nl

Norway
The Confraternity of St James, Norway
www.pilegrim.no

Poland
Friends of the Way of St James in Poland
www.camino.net.pl

South Africa
The Confraternity of Saint James of
South Africa
www.csjofsa.za.org

Spain
The Federation of Spanish Associations
www.caminosantiago.org

Switzerland
Les Amis du Chemin de St Jaques Suisse
www.jakobsweg.ch

USA
American Pilgrims on the Camino
www.americanpilgrims.org

APPENDIX E
Useful contacts

Transport
Eurostar
tel 0343 218 6186 (UK reservations)
tel +33 (0)8 92 35 35 39 (F reservations)
tel 0344 822 5822 (UK baggage)
tel +33 (0)1 55 31 68 33 (F baggage)
www.eurostar.com

SNCF (French railways)
tel 0844 848 4064
www.oui-sncf.com

The man in seat 61 (rail travel information)
www.seat61.com

RENFE (Spanish railways)
www.renfe.com

Alsa bus (long distance buses in Spain)
www.alsa.com

Brittany Ferries
tel 0330 159 7000 (UK reservations)
www.brittany-ferries.co.uk

Cycling organisations
Cycling UK (formerly Cyclists' Touring Club)
Parklands, Railton Rd
Guildford
GU2 9JX
01483 238301 (membership)
08447 368458 (insurance)
www.cyclinguk.org

Bicigrino (association of cycle repair shops)
www.bicigrino.com

Maps and guides
Open Street Maps (online mapping)
www.openstreetmap.org

Stanfords
7 Mercer Walk
London
WC2H 9FA
tel 0207 836 1321
sales@stanfords.co.uk
www.stanfords.co.uk

The Map Shop
15 High St
Upton upon Severn
WR8 0HJ
tel 08000 854080 or 01684 593146
themapshop@btinternet.com
www.themapshop.co.uk

Accommodation
Hostel Bookers (independent hostel bookings)
www.hostelbookers.com

APPENDIX F
Language glossary

Useful words and phrases

English	Spanish (Castilian)
yes	sí
no	no
please	por favor
thank you	gracias
hello	hola
goodbye	adios
pilgrim	peregrino

Cycles and repairs

English	Spanish (Castilian)
bicycle	bicicleta ('bici')
brake	freno
cyclist	ciclista
inner tube	tubo interior
puncture	pinchado
tyre	neumático

On the trail

English	Spanish (Castilian)
bridge	puente
castle	castillo
cathedral	catedral
church	iglesia
cycle track	pista bicicletas
dirt road	camino de tierra
diversion	desvío

On the trail continued

English	Spanish (Castilian)
drinking water fountain	fuente agua potable
field	campo
forest/woods	bosque
footpath beside road	senda
hill	colina
monastery	monasterio
motorway	autopista
high point	alto de
mountain	montaña
no entry	sin entrada
one-way street	solo sentido
railway	ferrocarril
river	río
roundabout	rotonda, glorieta
station	estación
stream	arroyo
tourist information office	oficina de turismo
town hall	ayuntamiento
traffic light	semáforo
wayside cross	cruceiro

APPENDIX G
Spanish architectural styles

Romanesque
11th–12th centuries in northern Spain (it never reached southern Spain, which was still under Moorish rule)
- **Origin:** Arrived from France in the late 10th century, spread along the Camino into Spain by French religious orders (particularly reformed Benedictines from Cluny) and itinerant French craftsmen building cathedrals, monasteries and churches in French style
- **Key features:** Rounded arches, small windows, thick walls, heavy columns, recessed and carved door frames
- **Best examples:** The Palace of Navarre Kings in Estella (Stage 3), Santa María church in Eunate (side trip on Stage 3 road route), San Martin church in Frómista (Stage 9), San Isidoro basilica in León (Stage 11), Knights Templar castle in Ponferrada (Stage 13), part of Santiago cathedral but not the façade (Stage 18)

Mudéjar
12th century in central Spain, spreading south with the Reconquista, reaching southern Spain by the 15th century
- **Origin:** In areas freed from Muslim rule, Moorish styles and craftsmen influenced Christian architecture, resulting in crosses between first Moorish and Romanesque styles, later between Moorish and Gothic styles
- **Key features:** Use of brick, multiple windows, rounded chapels
- **Best examples:** San Tirso church in Sahagún (Stage 10)

Gothic
12th–15th centuries
- **Origin:** Originated in Central Europe, then succeeded Romanesque architecture in France and spread along the Camino in the 12th century
- **Key features:** Pointed arches, rib-vaulting, flying buttresses
- **Best examples:** Las Huelgas Monastery in Burgos (Stage 7), Burgos cathedral (Stage 7), León cathedral (Stage 11)

Renaissance
16th century
- **Origin:** Evolved in 15th-century Florence then spread throughout Europe. By the time it reached northern Spain the heyday of the Camino was over and little new building was underway
- **Key features:** Symmetrical design, orderly arrangement of columns, pilasters and lintels, semi-circular arches, domes
- **Best examples:** Guzmanes palace in León (Stage 11)

Plateresque
16th century
- **Origin:** An indigenous Spanish style but influenced by Italian Renaissance architecture. The name is derived from the Spanish for 'silversmith' and implies intricate decoration. Plateresque decorative elements (façades, alterpieces, chandeliers, etc) were often added to Gothic-style buildings
- **Key features:** Ornate decorative façades festooned with floral patterns, shields and fantastic creatures
- **Best examples:** Hospital del Rey in Burgos (Stage 7), façade of San Marcos (now a parador hotel) in León (Stage 11), Hostal dos Reyes Católicos (now also a parador hotel) in Santiago (Stage 18)

Baroque
17th–18th centuries
- **Origin:** Evolved in Rome as a style intended to reflect the glory of the Catholic Church. Spread through Catholic countries often by Jesuit orders. Often applied as redecoration or additions to existing older buildings
- **Key features:** Large interior spaces, barley sugar columns, use of sculptured angels and cherubs, gilding and bronzing of surfaces
- **Best examples:** Pamplona city hall (Stage 2), Santiago cathedral west façade (Stage 18)

Rococo
18th century
- **Origin:** Paris, then spread throughout Europe. Applied more to decoration than architecture
- **Key features:** Use of curved surfaces, shell shapes, asymmetrical designs, pale colours, interior mirrors
- **Best examples:** Not much in evidence on the Camino

Neoclassical (or Palladian)
18th–19th centuries
- **Origin:** Developed by northern Italian architect Andrea Palladio then spread across Europe mainly as a secular counter to Baroque
- **Key features:** Symmetrical rectilinear design, clean uncluttered lines, porticos and Greek-style columns with triangular pediments
- **Best examples:** Palacio de Raxoi in Santiago (Stage 18)

Neo-Gothic (or Gothic revival)
19th century
- **Origin:** London, then spread across Europe
- **Key features:** Gothic design (see above) but often using newer materials and techniques
- **Best examples:** Not much in evidence on the Camino although neo-Gothic elements were incorporated into Spanish modernism

Modernism
Late 19th–early 20th centuries
- **Origin:** Developed by Catalan architect Antoni Gaudí blending elements of Mudéjar and neo-Gothic styles
- **Key features:** Preference for curves over straight lines, asymmetry, high level of decoration, use of ceramic tiles, attention to detail
- **Best examples:** Casa Botines in León (Stage 11), the Episcopal palace in Astorga (Stage 12); Barcelona (not on the Camino) has many examples of this style

LISTING OF CICERONE GUIDES

BRITISH ISLES CHALLENGES, COLLECTIONS AND ACTIVITIES

The Big Rounds
The Book of the Bivvy
The Book of the Bothy
The C2C Cycle Route
The Mountains of England and Wales:
    Vol 1 Wales
    Vol 2 England
The National Trails
Walking The End to End Trail
Cycling Land's End to John o' Groats

SCOTLAND

Ben Nevis and Glen Coe
Cycle Touring in Northern Scotland
Cycling in the Hebrides
Great Mountain Days in Scotland
Mountain Biking in Southern and Central Scotland
Mountain Biking in West and North West Scotland
Not the West Highland Way Scotland
Scotland's Best Small Mountains
Scotland's Mountain Ridges
Skye's Cuillin Ridge Traverse
The Borders Abbeys Way
The Great Glen Way
The Great Glen Way Map Booklet
The Hebridean Way
The Hebrides
The Isle of Mull
The Isle of Skye
The Skye Trail
The Southern Upland Way
The Speyside Way
The Speyside Way Map Booklet
The West Highland Way
The West Highland Way Map Booklet
Walking Ben Lawers, Rannoch and Atholl
Walking in the Cairngorms
Walking in the Pentland Hills
Walking in the Scottish Borders
Walking in the Southern Uplands
Walking in Torridon
Walking Loch Lomond and the Trossachs
Walking on Arran
Walking on Harris and Lewis
Walking on Jura, Islay and Colonsay
Walking on Rum and the Small Isles
Walking on the Orkney and Shetland Isles
Walking on Uist and Barra
Walking the Cape Wrath Trail

Walking the Corbetts
    Vol 1 South of the Great Glen
    Vol 2 North of the Great Glen
Walking the Galloway Hills
Walking the Munros
    Vol 1 – Southern, Central and Western Highlands
    Vol 2 – Northern Highlands and the Cairngorms
Winter Climbs Ben Nevis and Glen Coe
Winter Climbs in the Cairngorms

NORTHERN ENGLAND TRAILS

Hadrian's Wall Path
Hadrian's Wall Path Map Booklet
The Coast to Coast Walk
The Coast to Coast Walk Map Booklet
The Pennine Way
The Pennine Way Map Booklet
Walking the Dales Way
Walking the Dales Way Map Booklet
Walking the Tour of the Lake District

NORTH EAST ENGLAND, YORKSHIRE DALES AND PENNINES

Cycling in the Yorkshire Dales
Great Mountain Days in the Pennines
Mountain Biking in the Yorkshire Dales
St Oswald's Way and St Cuthbert's Way
The Cleveland Way and the Yorkshire Wolds Way
The Cleveland Way Map Booklet
The North York Moors
The Reivers Way
The Teesdale Way
Trail and Fell Running in the Yorkshire Dales
Walking in County Durham
Walking in Northumberland
Walking in the North Pennines
Walking in the Yorkshire Dales: North and East
Walking in the Yorkshire Dales: South and West

NORTH WEST ENGLAND AND THE ISLE OF MAN

Cycling the Pennine Bridleway
Cycling the Reivers Route
Cycling the Way of the Roses
Hadrian's Cycleway
Isle of Man Coastal Path
The Lancashire Cycleway
The Lune Valley and Howgills

Walking in Cumbria's Eden Valley
Walking in Lancashire
Walking in the Forest of Bowland and Pendle
Walking on the Isle of Man
Walking on the West Pennine Moors
Walks in Silverdale and Arnside

LAKE DISTRICT

Cycling in the Lake District
Great Mountain Days in the Lake District
Joss Naylor's Lakes, Meres and Waters of the Lake District
Lake District Winter Climbs
Lake District: High Level and Fell Walks
Lake District: Low Level and Lake Walks
Mountain Biking in the Lake District
Outdoor Adventures with Children – Lake District
Scrambles in the Lake District – North
Scrambles in the Lake District – South
The Cumbria Way
Trail and Fell Running in the Lake District
Walking the Lake District Fells:
    Borrowdale
    Buttermere
    Coniston
    Keswick
    Langdale
    Mardale and the Far East
    Patterdale
    Wasdale

DERBYSHIRE, PEAK DISTRICT AND MIDLANDS

Cycling in the Peak District
Dark Peak Walks
Scrambles in the Dark Peak
Walking in Derbyshire
Walking in the Peak District – White Peak East
Walking in the Peak District – White Peak West

SOUTHERN ENGLAND

20 Classic Sportive Rides in South East England
20 Classic Sportive Rides in South West England
Cycling in the Cotswolds
Mountain Biking on the North Downs
Mountain Biking on the South Downs
Suffolk Coast and Heath Walks

For full information on all our guides,
books and eBooks,
visit our website:
www.cicerone.co.uk

CICERONE

Trust Cicerone to guide your next adventure,
wherever it may be around the world...

Discover guides for hiking, mountain walking, backpacking,
trekking, trail running, cycling and mountain biking, ski touring,
climbing and scrambling in Britain, Europe and worldwide.

Connect with Cicerone online and find inspiration.

- buy books and ebooks
- articles, advice and trip reports
- podcasts and live events
- GPX files and updates
- regular newsletter

cicerone.co.uk